Nayef R.F. Al-Rodhan (ed.)

Policy Briefs on the *Transcultural* Aspects of Security and Stability

Policy Briefs on the *Transcultural* Aspects of Security and Stability

edited by
Nayef R.F. Al-Rodhan

LIT

∞

Gedruckt auf alterungsbeständigem Werkdruckpapier entsprechend
ANSI Z3948 DIN ISO 9706

Bibliographic information published by the Deutsche Nationalbibliothek
The Deutsche Nationalbibliothek lists this publication in the Deutsche Nationalbibliografie; detailed bibliographic data are available in the Internet at http://dnb.d-nb.de.

ISBN-10: 3-03735-148-9 (Switzerland)
ISBN-10: 3-8258-0179-9 (Germany)

ISBN-13: 978-3-03735-148-2 (Switzerland)
ISBN-13: 978-3-8258-0179-3 (Germany)

Dufourstr. 31
CH-8008 Zürich
Tel. +41 (0) 44-251 75 05
Fax +41 (0) 44-251 75 06
e-Mail: zuerich@lit-verlag.ch
http://www.lit-verlag.ch

LIT VERLAG Dr. W. Hopf
Berlin
Dietrich-Bonhoeffer-Haus
Ziegelstr. 30
D-10177 Berlin

Auslieferung:
Deutschland: LIT Verlag Fresnostr. 2, D-48159 Münster
Tel. +49 (0) 2 51/620 32 - 22, Fax +49 (0) 2 51/922 60 99, e-Mail: vertrieb@lit-verlag.de

Distributed in the UK by: Global Book Marketing, 99B Wallis Rd, London, E9 5LN
Phone: +44 (0) 20 8533 5800 – Fax: +44 (0) 1600 775 663
http://www.centralbooks.co.uk/acatalog/search.html

Distributed in North America by:

Transaction Publishers
New Brunswick (U.S.A.) and London (U.K.)

Transaction Publishers
Rutgers University
35 Berrue Circle
Piscataway, NJ 08854

Phone: +1 (732) 445 - 2280
Fax: + 1 (732) 445 - 3138
for orders (U. S. only):
toll free (888) 999 - 6778
e-mail:
orders@transactionspub.com

CONTENTS

Acknowledgements

I would like to take this opportunity to extend my gratitude to those who have assisted me in the publication of this work.

I am grateful to Ambassador Gérard Stoudmann for his wisdom and guidance; Dr. Fred Tanner for his mentoring and his insights; Paul Clark for his research assistance; Bethany Webster for her administrative and drafting assistance.

Thank you also to Lisa Watanabe and Ekaterina Rykovanova for their dedication to our program and for their contributions to this work.

Of course, we are also grateful to all of our authors who have made this work possible through their insightful contributions. The program is also indebted to our editors, Curtis Budden, Jean Callaghan, and Christopher Findlay.

Finally, this publication could not have been possible without the collaboration with the faculty and staff of the Geneva Centre for Security Policy. The program is grateful for their continued support.

NOTES ON THE CONTRIBUTORS

Nayef R.F. Al-Rodhan, M.D., PhD., is Senior Scholar in Geostrategy and the Director of the Program on the Geopolitical Implications of Globalization and Transnational Security at the Geneva Centre for Security Policy, Geneva, Switzerland.

Fraser Cameron is Director of EuroFocus-Brussels and Senior Advisor to the European Policy Centre, Brussels, Belgium.

Katja M. Flückiger is Academic Assistant at the Geneva Centre for Security Policy, Geneva, Switzerland.

Graeme Herd is Joint Course Director of the International Training Course in Security Policy at the Geneva Centre for Security Policy, Geneva, Switzerland.

Slobodan Djajic is Professor of International Economics at the Graduate Institute of International Studies, Geneva, Switzerland.

Mark Sheetz is Faculty Member at the Geneva Centre for Security Policy, Geneva, Switzerland.

Anne Deighton is Faculty Member at the Geneva Centre for Security Policy, Geneva, Switzerland and University Lecturer at the University of Oxford, United Kingdom.

Andreas Busch is Reader in European Politics at the University of Oxford, United Kingdom.

Miriam Ahmed Fugfugosh is Course Coordinator for the European Training Course in Security Policy and Exercises and Skill Development Training Officer at the Geneva Centre for Security Policy, Geneva, Switzerland.

Thierry Tardy is Course Director of the European Training Course in Security Policy at the Geneva Centre for Security Policy, Geneva, Switzerland.

Victor-Yves Ghebali is Professor of Political Science at the Graduate Institute of International Studies, Geneva, Switzerland.

Marc Finaud is Faculty Member at the Geneva Centre for Security Policy, Geneva, Switzerland.

CHAPTER 1

THE TRANSCULTURAL POLICY BRIEF SERIES

NAYEF R.F. AL-RODHAN

Dr. Nayef R.F. Al-Rodhan is Senior Scholar in Geostrategy and Director of the Program on the Geopolitical Implications of Globalization and Transnational Security at the Geneva Centre for Security Policy, Geneva, Switzerland

Introduction

The Geneva Centre for Security Policy (GCSP) policy brief series was created in order to assess the challenges, dilemmas, implications, and future trends of various policies related to globalization and security. The Program on the Geopolitical Implications of Globalization and Transnational Security, which publishes the series, is based on both a thematic and a policy perspective. This series represents an analysis and assessment of current issues that are either presently being discussed as part of policy-making agendas, or will be increasingly important issues in the future.

The subjects discussed have been selected for the way in which they illustrate the links between globalization and security. The authors come from diverse backgrounds and offer unique expertise as well as a dynamic approach to the topics discussed.

The topics discussed and approach used in each of these briefs represent the personal perspectives of the authors and do not necessarily represent the perspective of GSCP or the program. Rather, each brief has been produced at the sole discretion of the authors. Consequently, it has become necessary to add the perspectives and opinions of the program as well as my own. Therefore, each brief is followed by an editorial based on the brief and the ideas and arguments put forth within it.

The papers have undergone the usual academic peer review process. We feel that they have taken on a unique shape that illuminates a unified and consistent link between the various policy issues and recommendations. Each editorial outlines eight problems and recommendations on how to resolve them or adapt to the constraints they create.

While some of the problems may seem rather obvious and the recommendations in some instances unrealistic, we have proposed them in order to state what needs to be done and to point out the issues that do exist, rather than to work within a framework of assumptions. By eliminating necessary courses of action because they are unrealistic due to certain political, social, or economic restraints, we might suppress discussions and decisions that would prove useful for promoting further security and stability. In this way, recommendations that are essential for international and national systems are put forth for further discussion and analysis.

The formal presentation of the editorial pieces is also very illustrative. The editorial circle vividly expresses that each of these dilemmas and recommendations exists within the realm of other dilemmas and recommendations. The circle attempts to demonstrate the connections between the various dilemmas as well as their relationship to the subsequent recommendations. Visually, the circle provides the template to communicate this aspect of the policy-making process while illustrating a number of dilemmas and recommendations simultaneously. The diagram creates a concise and specific conceptualization of the policies being assessed and can serve as a guide for lecturing, discussions, and analysis well beyond this publication.

Policy Briefs on the Transcultural Aspects of Security and Stability

This edition of the policy brief series specifically focuses on the transcultural aspects of policy making for greater security and stability. The chapters of this volume will explore topics such as migration, ethics and civil liberties, peace operations, and the role of the United Nations (UN). These topics can all be seen as pieces of the human aspect of globalization, either through the direct impact of the subject (migration, for instance) or by virtue of their development and influence (the UN). The focus in each of these briefs is on the human security perspective, highlighting problems of culture, ethnic tensions, and the resulting potential for insecurity and instability.

As illustrated in the briefs dealing with the printing of the Mohammed cartoons, United States hegemony, remittances, and the potential accession of Turkey to the European Union, as well as in a number of others, the significance of human development, cultural clashes, political partisanship, and potential racially motivated decisions and policies is becoming more clearly evident. Throughout these briefs, the issues that are found at the individual and societal levels are clearly identified as historical, current, or future sources of insecurity and instability. Each brief addresses these problems differently, but all conclude with recommendations that states may follow in order to minimize the deleterious impact of any of these factors on transnational security.

The implications for the security and stability of nation-states, cultures, and the idea of creating avenues towards peace and understanding are given prominence in each of these briefs. The dynamism and information found throughout this publication will provide the reader with a unique perspective on each of these topics, with concrete solutions for individual states as well as regions and the entire international system.

CHAPTER 2

TRANSCULTURAL ISSUES, GLOBALIZATION, AND GLOBAL SECURITY

FRASER CAMERON

Dr. Fraser Cameron is Director of EuroFocus-Brussels and Senior Advisor to the European Policy Centre, Brussels, Belgium

Abstract
There is now a real danger that Samuel Huntington's famous prophecy of a "clash of civilizations" will become a reality.[1] *The United States' global war on terror has had extremely negative consequences for attempts to promote transcultural understanding. In America, and to a lesser extent in Europe, there is mounting evidence of Islamophobia. Many in the West are profoundly ignorant of the contributions made by non-Western cultures to the modern world. This ignorance and the manner in which the US is engaged in the war on terror have profound implications for global security.*[2] *For reasons of space, this policy brief focuses primarily on the transcultural issues raised by the West's response to Islamic fundamentalism.*

1. Policy Challenges

The defining characteristic of today's world is interdependence. A United States (US) farming bill has implications for Chile, Chad, and Canada. European Union (EU) tariffs affect Thailand, Tanzania, and Turkey. Climate change, HIV/AIDS, and Asian bird flu affect every country. The omnipresent media bring images of suffering and conflict to our screens, prompting rock stars to engage in global campaigns to help eradicate poverty. Globalization has affected almost every country but not always in a positive manner. To many living outside Europe and North America, it looks uncomfortably like Westernization, or Americanization, since the US is now the sole superpower with a dominant military, economic, and cultural footprint in the global order. Many of the most visible cultural expressions of globalization are American: Coca-Cola, McDonald's, Nike, Microsoft.

According to the World Bank, the poorest 20 percent of the world's population share 1.4 percent of global income, compared to 85 percent for the richest 20 percent. To some, globalization is more code for global pillage than global village. In terms of global security, terrorism tops the list for the US and Europe. But for most of the world's population living on less than a dollar a day, there are very different security concerns: food, shelter, clean water, basic medical and educational facilities for their children. According to Hanan Ashwari, "the distortions and inequities of superimposing a Western economic model on developing countries and non-Western cultures and the built-in discriminatory practices of global economic institutions are producing a potent counter-culture seeking rectification and challenging prevailing norms."[3] The West pays lip service to the cries of the South and continues to spend obscene sums on military capacities compared to development assistance.[4] The Pentagon spends more than the annual United Nations (UN) budget in 48 hours.

The past few centuries have seen the growing dominance of Western culture, epitomized by the spread of Western empires, the adoption of the Gregorian calendar, and the universal business suit for men. There is little appreciation in the West of the enormous contribution to global development made by other cultures and civilizations. In many Muslim countries, there is growing resentment at Western culture and Western double standards in dealing with issues such as the Israel-Palestine conflict, Iran's nuclear program, and the selective approach to democracy promotion in the wider Middle East. The American-led attacks on two Muslim countries, Afghanistan and Iraq, have added further fuel to the flames. Four British Muslims were so angered at British involvement in the war that they carried out a series of suicide bombings in London in July 2005.[5]

The hostile response of the Islamic world to the publication of cartoons featuring the prophet Mohammed in Danish and other European newspapers demonstrates how quickly passions can be aroused. This led to what Danish Prime Minister Anders Rasmussen described as "the worst crisis in Danish foreign policy for 50 years" and prompted the EU's foreign policy chief, Javier Solana, to undertake a hasty, fence-building visit to the Middle East.[6] There was similar outrage previously about the publication of Salmon Rushdie's novel *The Satanic Verses* and the BBC's screening of a film, *Death of a Princess*, about women in Saudi Arabia. The murder of Dutch filmmaker Theo van Gogh following his critical film about the treatment of Muslim women demonstrates the intensity of such passions.[7] This attack has led to a fundamental reappraisal of Dutch attitudes towards Muslim immigrants and the criteria for Dutch citizenship. There are now strict tests about Dutch history, society, and language.

Access to information and the ability to influence its dissemination are key factors in any analysis of transcultural issues. On the one hand, the communications revolution, and especially the Internet, has had a considerable leveling influence. On the other hand, the major media outlets are firmly in the grip of a small number of powerful corporations and individuals with a very "Davos" view of global trends.[8]

In light of these developments, there are important policy challenges facing the West. How can the principles of free speech be upheld and defended when this can lead to what may appear as blasphemy in other countries? How can the widespread impression of double standards and hypocrisy be avoided or mitigated? How can intercultural dialogue be promoted? How can the very real threat of Islamic fundamentalist terrorism be dealt with? How can a genuine consensus on global threats to security be achieved? As United Kingdom (UK) Prime Minister Tony Blair asserted in a speech on March 21, 2006: "this is not a clash between civilisations. It is a clash about civilisation."[9]

2. Responses

The response of the West to the above challenges has been divided. A vast increase in US military spending has been accompanied by a greater European emphasis on human security and conflict prevention. The concept of the West has become looser since the end of the Cold War and the collapse of the Soviet Union. Francis Fukuyama's thesis about the end of history has not been vindicated.[10] The US and the EU, the twin pillars of the West during the Cold War era, are drifting apart on many issues, including threat perceptions and appropriate responses. There are major differences on violence and gun control, on health care and social security. Above all, it is the religious divide that separates Europe and America. While Europe is mostly secular, the US is deeply religious, and this religious attachment makes itself felt across the spectrum of policy issues. Despite these differences, there remain common values in terms of attachment to democracy, the rule of law, and market economies. But even these values are called into question by American behavior in Guantánamo and Abu Ghraib.

Although most Europeans distance themselves from the policies of the Bush administration, Europe is still lumped together with the US to form "the West" in many parts of the world. For example, both the US and the EU have been strongly criticized by many developing countries for their protectionist agricultural policies.[11] The West continues its stranglehold on international institutions such as the UN Security Council, the G8, the International Monetary Fund (IMF), and the World Bank. The West was, however, split on the wisdom and legality of the Iraq war. Dominated by neo-conservatives suffering from an excess of hubris and a lack of basic knowledge about other countries and cultures, the first Bush administration actively sought war against Iraq in 2002-03. The lack of preparations for the post-war period are quite staggering, reflecting the belief of the neo-conservatives that Iraqis would greet US troops as democratic heroes and be ready to open a McDonald's on every street corner. The lack of Arabic speakers, the disinterest in the looting of Iraqi museums, and the failure to secure basic services for the civilian population have all been heavily criticized by observers closely involved in the post-war period.[12]

In Afghanistan, the US military operation *Enduring Freedom* has had limited success in eradicating the Taliban and little success in winning hearts and minds. The Central Intelligence Agency (CIA) has admitted to having only a handful of Arabic speakers and has embarked on a crash recruitment program to find more. Observers have also been critical of the lack of intelligence officials with training in other cultures and languages. Only belatedly has Secretary of Defense Donald Rumsfeld seemed to recognize the importance of the public-relations battle. The 2006 US National Security Strategy states that the US is only at the start of a lengthy war on terrorism and that ultimately it is a battle for hearts and minds. But one sentence in a policy document plus the appointment of one of Bush's closest advisors, Karen Hughes, as the head of PR for the State Department do not constitute an adequate response to the problem. The US has also pushed for "free and fair" elections as a remedy for terrorism but seems reluctant to recognize the results if the "wrong" party wins, e.g., Hamas.

3. Dilemmas

The US is keen to have Europe, and as many other allies as possible, actively support its No. 1 priority: the war on terror. For Europe, a central dilemma is to what extent it wishes to be perceived as being allied with the US in the war on terror. Europeans do not use the phrase *war on terror* but speak rather of the *fight against terrorism*. Several European states were dealing with ruthless terrorist groups long before 9/11 and understand that there is no military response to terrorism.[13] The steadily increasing American demand for improved security is having major repercussions on travel. In addition to requiring visas, most visitors are fingerprinted and have their eyes scanned, and their personal data is passed to some twenty US agencies even before arrival in America. Human rights groups are concerned about these developments, while business is concerned at the delays and costs of the extra security procedures. The global image of Fortress America is highly damaging to the US. A central dilemma for the US is how to get the balance right.

Another dilemma is how to deal with failed states that may provide breeding grounds for terrorists or criminals. Neither the US nor the West as a whole can invade, conquer, and administer all the countries that fall into this category. Yet the West cannot ignore what is happening in these states, as chaos and civil war often lead to genocide (Rwanda), rampant militias (Sudan), and organized crime (Kosovo). Despite open condemnation of nation-building by the first Bush administration, it is clear that this is what the US, the EU, and international organizations will be doing for some considerable time. The new UN Peacebuilding Commission provides an opportunity for the major players to operate in a more coherent manner.

Iran poses a particular dilemma. In Iranian eyes, it is justified in seeking to develop a nuclear capability because of its precarious geographical position (surrounded by nuclear-weapons states), because it has had chemical weapons used against it (by Iraq under Saddam Hussein), and because it has a sovereign right to do so. In its approach to Iran, the US has chosen a policy of isolation and sanctions that has led nowhere. The EU has preferred to seek a negotiated resolution of the nuclear issue, but it clearly does not have sufficient carrots to offer Iran. Only the US has the carrots that Iran desires (regime recognition, security guarantees), yet it refuses to talk directly with Tehran, blinded by memories of the 1979 hostage crisis and unceasing Israeli pleas about the threat posed by Iran. There is never a mention in American discourse about US support for the overthrow of the democratically elected prime minister, Mohammad Mosaddeq, in 1954, of unstinting support for the repressive regime of the Shah, and backroom support for Saddam in fighting Iran. For most Iranians, this is a very selective approach to recent history.

4. Implications

There are no quick or easy solutions to the above-mentioned dilemmas. Indeed, in the short term, many security issues such as Iraq, Iran, Sudan, or the Arab-Israeli dispute may get worse before they get better. Demography is working against the West, including Israel. Like the Chinese, Al-Qaida has the patience to see developments in the longer term. The longer term for Western politicians is the next election. For the Western media, it is next week. It will be difficult for Western politicians to engage their publics to support policies for the longer term. Money can be found for missile defense, for building walls and fences, for new security measures at airports, but not for language training or cultural studies. Yet if there is no serious attempt to meet the legitimate concerns of the South (and in particular the plight of the Palestinians and a fair deal in the Doha round), the prospects for a reduction in terrorism will remain poor.

5. Future Scenarios

Global terrorism is here to stay, and it will remain the principal preoccupation of the US for many years. Because of the dominant position of the US on the global stage, this will have widespread implications. Even if Osama Bin Laden were captured or killed tomorrow, there is little doubt that the Al-Qaida network and its affiliates would continue their murderous attacks. Much will depend on whether there is another major terrorist attack in the US. If there were to be another attack, it could lead to even further hostility toward the Islamic world and even affect Muslims living in the US. America could lash out again if there was a connection to some state. It might also increase those voices calling for the US to return to its traditional posture of isolationism. Neither approach would be good for the US or the world at large. American interests are global and will remain global. It needs to continue to support an open, global trading system and to play by the international rulebook.

6. Policy Recommendations

Globalization is here to stay despite occasional Canute-like attempts at protectionism. Terrorists and criminals are adept at using global networks, while most governments fret over outdated concerns about sovereignty. It is instructive to consider the Franco-German reconciliation process with its support for a unique form of sharing sovereignty in Europe as an example of tolerance and statesmanship. There are perhaps some lessons here for other parts of the world such as the quest to improve Sino-Japanese relations.

A principal policy recommendation must be to promote a **stronger and more inclusive multilateral system.** An inclusive, fair, rules-based international system is the best public good on offer. The problem is how to ensure fairness when the global power system is so heavily skewed in favor of one nation that is highly dubious about the role and legitimacy of international organizations.

A second recommendation is to substantially **increase funding for foreign language and area studies,** especially Arabic and Chinese. American and European knowledge of Asia, for example, is woefully inadequate to deal with the "Asian century." Europeans have a longer history of involvement in the Middle East and Africa and thus a greater reserve of knowledge and experience to draw upon. But the advice of most experts was ignored in the run-up to the Iraq war. In Africa, commercial interests have usually won out over social and environmental interests.

A third recommendation is to support the new UN commitment regarding **the responsibility to protect.** The world cannot afford another Rwanda or Srebrenica. The UN Security Council must take its responsibilities for international security seriously and act in an even-handed manner.

A fourth recommendation is to **not neglect human rights** in fighting terrorism. As Cherie Blair wrote in the *Financial Times* on

March 2, 2006, "there can be no question of ignoring the fundamental question of human rights in the fight against terrorism." The Bush administration's treatment of prisoners at Guantánamo and elsewhere, and its reluctance to rule out the use of torture, has resulted in a severe loss of moral authority.

A fifth recommendation is to implement the proposals in the **Arab Human Development Report**.[14] This outstanding report was written by Arab scholars who pointed to major deficiencies in the political and economic structures of Arab countries. Their report highlighted the importance of democracy, human rights, and education of females.

The final recommendation is to **strengthen fora for transcultural dialogue**. Current efforts such as the Anna Lindh Foundation's support for trans-Mediterranean dialogue in Alexandria and the Turkish-Spanish initiative for interfaith dialogue need to be multiplied.[15]

References

---

[1] S. Huntington, *The Clash of Civilizations, and the Remaking of the World Order* (New York: Simon & Schuster, 1996).

[2] See, for example, the US National Security Strategy of September 2002, available at www.state.org and updated in March 2006. For an assessment of the latest version, see A. Lieven, "There is Menace in America's Policy of Prevention," *Financial Times*, March 20, 2006.

[3] "Globalisation and its impact on issues of power and sovereignty," available at http://www.bbc.co.uk/worldservice/people/features/world_lectures.

[4] See the World Bank website at www.worldbank.org. Military expenditures are available at www.sipri.org.

[5] The London bombings provoked an intense debate in the UK about the nature of its multicultural society and the question of 'identity' for Muslims living there. See, for example, R. Norton-Taylor, "There's No Such Thing As Total Security," *The Guardian*, August, 19, 2005. Also see www.opendemocracy.net.

[6] For Solana's remarks on February 13, 2006, in Jeddah, where he met with Ekmeleddin Ihsanoglu, secretary general of the Organization of the Islamic Conference, see www.ue.eu.int/solana.

[7] The outrage of Muslims at the publication of the cartoons in the European media is analyzed by T. Ali, "Comment & Debate: This is the Real Outrage: Amid the Cartoon Furore, Danish Imams Ignore the Tragedies Suffered by Muslims Across the World," *The Guardian*, February 13, 2006, Neil Acherson in *A Carnival of Stupidity,* March 6, 2006, available at www.opendemocracy.net; K. Amayreh in *Islam and the West: Conflict or Cohesion?,* March 4, 2006, http://english.aljazeera.net.

[8] It is worth noting that both Fox and Microsoft made concessions to the Chinese authorities in order to be able to enter the Chinese market.

[9] See www.number-10.gov.uk for the full text of the Blair speech.

[10] F. Fukuyama, *The End of History* (New York: Penguin, 1993).

[11] See, for example, the trade section of www.oxfam.org.uk, www.ethicaltrade.org, www.forumsocialmundial.org.be/eng/index.asp.

[12] G. Parker, *The Assassins' Gate: America in Iraq* (New York: Farrar, Straus and Giroux, 2005); J. Benjamin and S. Simon, *The Next Attack: The Failure of the War on Terror and a Strategy for Getting it Right* (New York: Henry Holt, 2005).

[13] The lengthy, patient, essentially non-military approach by the British and Spanish governments towards the IRA and ETA led to permanent cease-fires.

[14] This report has been published a number of times by the United Nations Development Programme, however, the most recent report was released in 2005. For all of the reports including the most recent version, please see https://unp.un.org/.

[15] Prince Charles added his weight to the cause in a noteworthy speech at the Al-Azhar University in Cairo on March 21, 2006, when he called for greater understanding between the three great Abrahamic faiths of Islam, Judaism, and Christianity.

CHAPTER 3

EDITORIAL OF POLICY BRIEF ON TRANSCULTURAL ISSUES, GLOBALIZATION, AND GLOBAL SECURITY

NAYEF R.F. AL-RODHAN

Dr. Nayef R.F. Al-Rodhan is Senior Scholar in Geostrategy and Director of the Program on the Geopolitical Implications of Globalization and Transnational Security at the Geneva Centre for Security Policy, Geneva, Switzerland

1. Review and Critique

The current global security situation does not provide an ideal setting for improving intercultural understanding. France recently dealt with such transcultural issues when riots broke out in November 2005 as a result of the accidental electrocution of two teenagers as they hid in an electric power station believing they were being chased by police. One major aspect of the debate surrounding how to handle transcultural tensions is the role that Muslims play in Western societies. More specifically for the purposes of this brief, it is important to look at the transcultural issues that have been raised as a result of the West's reaction to Islamic fundamentalism. As the war on terror polarizes countries and societies, these issues and tensions enter the foreground as a genuine security issue. Young Muslims are becoming frustrated by the way in which they are grouped together with those that wish harm to the West, such as the individuals that orchestrated the London bombings in July 2005. Others find that they are born and raised in a European country and yet are not accepted as being Dutch, German, French, or Spanish due to their Islamic heritage.

Some countries are responding to this frustration by tightening their citizenship laws. One prominent example is the Netherlands, which tightened its citizenship rules as a direct result of the murder of filmmaker Theo van Gogh in 2004. Instead of furthering integration, however, such a reaction will only create more barriers that will need to be overcome.

In his policy brief "Transcultural Issues, Globalization, and Global Security," Dr. Fraser Cameron examines the current state challenges and dilemmas in terms of transcultural issues and tensions.[1] He focuses on the "transcultural issues raised by the West's response to Islamic fundamentalism." Dr. Cameron explains, to say the least, that the response has been divided. This divided response is certainly also a result of how countries have evolved, for instance whether it is a country which is accustomed to having immigrants working and living among its population as in the case of the United States (US) or if it is a country where this is a recent phenomenon such as in countries like France. This is an important point that is not addressed in the scope of the paper. Rather, the brief presents Western countries as a kind of group and outlines the challenges that this presents for the governing bodies of the European Union (EU). This is becoming especially prominent as the EU tries to distance itself from United States policies, which it is finding to be a near-impossible task.

While the brief focuses on a few state challenges without directly linking them to transcultural issues and challenges, overall, the review of the issue was cohesive and succinct. It provides a clear trajectory of where policies *may* be headed in a few years' time and what policies need to focus on in order to make the "clash of civilizations" a thing of the past.

2. Dilemmas and Our Recommendations

Transcultural issues and the multicultural nature of societies create profound policy dilemmas for states. The quandaries raised by these dilemmas, as well as the policy decisions states have to take in response, are very sensitive and important issues, as they can have a widespread impact on state security. This is evident in the recent example of the international reaction to the publication of cartoons depicting the Prophet Mohammed in Western media.

Presented below are eight dilemmas and corresponding recommendations for appropriate policy reactions at the state level.

While it is not necessary to explain the importance of all of the dilemmas and recommendations, it is worth expanding on those that could have the most resounding impact. The first dilemma is important for any state dealing with these issues. In attempting to maintain state and human security in democratic societies, the preservation of civil liberties is non-negotiable. Second, any policy in this area should ensure that the peaceful majority of any immigrant population does not fall victim to stereotypes that may risk linking them to the radical minority. Politicians must refrain from employing fear and xenophobic statements against groups or cultures for political reasons. The last dilemma that should be noted is the problem that immigrants face in terms of choosing between their native religious and cultural identity and the national identity of their host country.

State reactions to each of these dilemmas must be clearly formulated and justified, as well as encompassing and inclusive, in order to avoid angering large groups of immigrant and culturally diverse communities. If these recommendations are implemented in state security policies, there must be some form of accountability and regulation. The execution of such policies must ensure efficiency while protecting civil liberties. In addition, freedom of expression should be coupled with responsibility, and states should enact anti-hate legislation to protect these immigrant and minority communities.

Immigrant communities, through their representatives, must demonstrate loyalty to their adoptive country and contribute to its security and prosperity. If they have concerns about world events or about their host country's policy regarding issues that they care about, such as their culture or religion, their concerns should be demonstrated through the use of peaceful petitioning and the use of the mechanisms of democracy, including the electoral process and through free expression. In turn, host countries should facilitate the participation of immigrant communities in the democratic process. They should acknowledge their grievances and contributions and promote their inclusion and prosperity. Furthermore, through responsible and inclusive political statements, policies, media, and education, the state should avoid the demonization and exclusion of these groups. On the foreign policy front, host countries should strive to contribute to global justice and equality through effective, multilateral international policies that promote the resolution of conflicts around the globe; they should strive to implement policies that will not be perceived by immigrant communities as double standards and intentionally unjust.

Finally, there needs to be encouragement of the state on society towards the process of globalization instead of a fight against it. The forces in the globalization process that promote cosmopolitanism and diversity should be seen as strengths and viewed as a means toward furthering global security and harmony.

When applied, these recommendations will contribute to easing transcultural tensions and provide an environment where immigrant communities can also prosper while contributing to the welfare of the state instead of being victims or a cause of uncertainty and chaos.

3. Conclusion

The issues surrounding multicultural and transcultural issues are certainly not new; however, some of these issues need to be dealt with more effectively at the societal and state levels in order to make immigrants and communities feel more secure and stable. Without this, an environment of peace, security, and stability will never be achieved on a larger scale. States are certainly facing the dilemmas presented here, and they are not easily rectified, even by the suggestions that have been provided. States have to find the right balance between the opposing choices in these dilemmas, which will take time and patience. Only then will these transcultural issues truly start to see marked improvement at the societal level and will ultimately lead to a more secure international system.

References

[1] For the brief in its entirety, please see Chapter 2.

CHAPTER 4

XENOPHOBIA, MEDIA STEREOTYPING, AND THEIR ROLE IN GLOBAL INSECURITY

KATJA M. FLÜCKIGER

Ms. Katja M. Flückiger is Academic Assistant at the Geneva Centre for Security Policy, Geneva, Switzerland

Abstract
Xenophobic stereotyping in the media is a common and increasing phenomenon. Immigrants, asylum seekers, refugees, Muslims, and Sinti and Roma are often represented as a threat to the security of longer-established populations; they are systematically portrayed as perpetrators of crime but appear very seldom as actors in other news genres. Exposure to these stereotypes often influence readers and viewers to support policy measures directed against these minorities and has led to discrimination against them, often subtle, sometimes going as far as physical violence. An extreme form of xenophobic stereotyping has been the propaganda spread by so-called hate radios that have spurred communal conflict. Another contemporary form of xenophobia in media are hate sites on the Internet. Initiatives to combat these forms of xenophobia, stereotyping, and discrimination face the challenge of not curtailing freedom of speech. Many media organizations have undertaken projects to increase awareness of these problems, to train journalists, and to increase the access of minorities to mainstream media, so that their voices are heard. However, these initiatives have to become more widely known and applied, and especially tabloid media have to be targeted. In addition, there should be a focus on education in media literacy in schools.

1. Policy Challenges

It is through the media that we learn most of what we know or believe we know about world affairs and politics, not through personal experience or contacts. Stereotyping in the media is as old as the media itself. A stereotype can be defined as "a standardized mental picture that is held in common by members of a group and that represents an oversimplified opinion, prejudiced attitude, or uncritical judgment."[1] In today's media, especially in Europe, there are several groups that are regularly, and even systematically, stereotyped: immigrants, asylum seekers, and refugees; Roma and Sinti; and, increasingly since 9/11, Muslims. This phenomenon contributes to discrimination of these groups of people, as well as, ironically, to a feeling of insecurity among the native (and/or Christian population). Xenophobic stereotyping in the media can go as far as to constitute so-called hate speech and to contribute, if not unleash, armed communal conflict, even genocide.

Various studies have analyzed the way immigrants, asylum seekers, and refugees are portrayed in today's media. Migrants appear more frequently in certain news genres, such as crime news, than others, and these reports often follow a standard script that shows them in a negative light, as the culprits rather than the victims.[2] This has "become systematic and leads to ethnicisation or racialisation of crime"[3] and has reached a degree where, in public discourse, immigration issues are discussed solely in terms of threats, crime, and alleged abuse of the welfare system. The reasons for immigration and the everyday living conditions of migrants are totally left out of the debate. The frequent association of migrants with crime "may reinforce the belief or perception that negative behaviour is inextricably linked to the ethnic identity features of the individual's group belonging."[4] Research on British media, which can, in large part, be applied to many other countries in Europe and North America, has found "inaccurate and provocative use of language," including "meaningless and derogatory terms" and overwhelming focus on the number of people entering the country, with numbers frequently being unsourced, exaggerated, or inadequately explained, with no contextual analysis of the relevance or meaning of the statistics being cited. Images are "dominated by the stereotype of the 'threatening young male'. Women and children are rarely seen, and stock images of groups of men trying to break into Britain are used repeatedly."[5] However, issues such as root causes for migration are largely absent. Moreover, British newspapers are astonishingly similar in their selection of themes when covering immigration issues, whatever their political affiliation.[6]

Media stereotyping and portraying a negative image of immigrants are not restricted to Western Europe or North America. Other examples include, for instance, Costa Rica (against immigrants from Nicaragua[7]), the South Caucasus, and South Africa: "coverage of international migration by the South African press has been largely anti-immigrant and unanalytical. Not all reportage is negative, and newspaper coverage would appear to be improving over time, but the overwhelming majority of the comprehensive collection of newspaper articles, editorials and letters to the editor surveyed for this research are negative about immigrants and immigration and are extremely unanalytical in nature, uncritically reproducing problematic statistics and assumptions about crossborder migration in the region."[8] Stereotyping of Muslims has been found in many media reports about 9/11, but one cannot speak of a generalized tendency in this regard: "In the period after September 11 certain media were identified as representing Muslims and Islam both negatively and stereotypically, sometimes as an almost necessary part of the reporting process, and (...) many of those that did change their attitudes or indeed participate in acts of aggression or violence towards Muslims, acted against visual identifiers that were essentially media-derived from the post-September 11 period."[9] Another report found that "the overall role played by the [North American] media in this situation is a negative one. The media consistently confuse 'Arab' with 'Muslim' and make outrageous categorizations and generalizations while neglecting differences. These almost comical errors are sometimes even committed by people presented as 'experts'. (...) However, during the post-September 11 period some media sectors also were responsible and accountable, while others sought to remain balanced and objective. Where positive and balanced attitudes were identified in the various media, the reporting was built on dialogue with the Muslim community and a critical engagement not only with Islam, but also with topics relating more directly to September 11. In those media, Muslim voices were given a platform to be heard and a cross section of opinion was discussed."[10] Media reactions in European countries after the bomb attacks on London in July 2005 were balanced in most countries; an effort was made to let Muslims and Muslim representatives speak themselves rather than only report about them.[11]

Why do we see this xenophobia and stereotyping in the media? One answer is that journalists' reporting simply mirrors their own prejudices. However, this is an unsatisfactory explanation. The realities of newsmaking must also be taken into account. Not every event or story has the same news value. Negativity is thought to sell well, and so is crime. Thus, there is an incentive for media professionals to organize, or "frame," reports around these themes.

Another reason commonly cited for negative portrayals and the focus on negative issues when reporting on immigrants is that the people used as sources are not immigrants themselves but rather authorities and officials, such as the police, who have an "innate" tendency to focus on security-related aspects and who are presented as credible, while immigrants, even when they are given time to speak, are presented as passive, reactive, and less credible. The overwhelming use of these sources and the lack of consideration of migrant organizations stems largely from the fact that there are not many strong connections between media professionals and migrants' representatives, and the latter often lack the resources and knowledge to make their points heard and to become agenda setters in the debate.

Research has shown that exposure to media shapes the way people think about groups:[12] a study on crime news in local media, for instance, showed that viewers exposed to a news report in which a picture of a suspected perpetrator was shown, and where it was mentioned whether he was black or white, became "more supportive of capital punishment, mandatory sentencing, and other deterrent measures and exposure to this version of the script also serve[d] to substantiate negative attitudes about racial minorities.... [F]or white viewers, a brief five-second exposure to a black perpetrator in the news is sufficient to stimulate small increases in the percentage of people who believe crime is caused by individual failings and who support punitive crime policies. In addition, exposure to a black perpetrator fosters the view that African-Americans are out of step with the cultural mainstream. On the other hand, the crime script has generally the opposite effect on African-American viewers."[13] Thus, exposure to stereotyping in the media does influence people's attitudes and does lead to xenophobia. It also makes people support policy measures that discriminate against the stereotyped.

Media stereotyping can in extreme cases also lead to more direct assaults on the security of those who are being stereotyped. *Radio des Mille Collines* in Rwanda is the best-known and most extreme example of hate speech on radio and its effects. But the media has also played a major negative role in other communal conflicts. *Fondation Hirondelle* and Radio Netherlands identified 11 countries where one or more "hate radios" – or TV stations – have operated, e.g., Serb TV in the former Yugoslavia.[14] The existence of these types of stations often seems to occur when controls on radio broadcasting are relaxed and can therefore potentially incite violence. Jack Snyder and Karen Ballentine have suggested that the "market place of ideas" that defines the idea of free media in Western societies only works if there are institutions in place that ensure the proper functioning of the market, otherwise elites, following the sudden liberalization of the media, have an incentive to play the ethnic or nationalist card, and the market will break up into ethnic segments as the elites are forced to engage in public debate in order to compete for mass allies in the struggle for power. However, many newly democratizing states lack such institutions to break up governmental and non-governmental monopolies, to professionalize journalism, and to create common public forums where individuals engage each other with diverse ideas under conditions in which erroneous arguments will be challenged.[15]

Jonathan Belman studied the hate propaganda used in Weimar Germany, Armenia, Rwanda, and the former Yugoslavia and found the following seven recurring messages that "consistently appear in the fiercest and most thorough campaigns of hate propaganda:" (1) the enemy is qualitatively different from us; (2) the enemy represents some great evil and that evilness is eternal; (3) the enemy has harmed us in the past with impunity; (4) the enemy has plans to harm us again in the future; (5) we are noble and deserving of good lives that the enemy would deny us; (6) the enemy is united so we must also be: those who undermine our unity are traitors or agents of the enemy; (7) this is the final battle; if we win we will move to a bright future free from the threat posed by enemy.

As mentioned above, another example of xenophobia in the media are so-called hate sites on the Internet, which disseminate various racist and other discriminating propaganda. The current number of Internet hate sites has been estimated at anywhere between 400 and over 2000.[16] Unlike the media reports discussed above, which sometimes involuntarily portray xenophobic images because of a lack of awareness on the part of journalists, the specific purpose of these sites is to propagate hatred and intolerance, even violence in some cases.[17] Given this intent, and also that the authors are individuals who cannot be reached through professional organizations, as is the case with most journalists, and because of the anarchic nature of the Internet and varying legislative frameworks regarding how far freedom of speech is protected, it is very difficult to shut down or eliminate these sites.

2. Responses

A number of initiatives by media organizations, states, international organizations, and migrant organizations have focused on reducing xenophobic stereotyping in the media, raising journalists' awareness of the issue, and improving access by migrants to the media to make their voices heard. The International Federation of Jurists (IFJ) launched its international working group against racism and xenophobia (IMRAX) in 1995. IMRAX has organized several conferences, introduced an award called "Celebration of Tolerance" in order to raise awareness, and has produced several handbooks. In Russia and countries of the former Yugoslavia, the IFJ has supported Reporting for Diversity, an initiative that has also produced handbooks and organized numerous seminars and other training for journalists and minority groups. IFJ's Media for Democracy is a project that has produced handbooks on diversity and on covering ethnic conflict in Africa and that has also organized training seminars. Online – More Colour in the Media is a European network that aims to improve the representation of ethnic minorities in the media. It has projects in the fields of employment, training, production, research and empowerment. [18]

In 1997, 31 codes of conduct for journalists existed in Europe. The IFJ Declaration of Principles was amended in 1986 to include an article stating, "The journalist shall be alert to the danger of discrimination being furthered by media, and shall do the utmost to avoid facilitating such discriminations based on, among other things, race, sex, sexual orientation, language, religion, political or other opinions, and national and social origins."[19] A number of press councils have also adopted codes on intolerance and hear complaints in that area. Many non-governmental organizations (NGOs) active in minority and immigration issues have formulated guidelines for journalists.

Several media outlets have introduced new guidelines and standards relating to recruitment in order to ensure that more journalists with a migration background are included among their staff, but these are fairly isolated incidents, rather than being a general trend. Such voluntary codes of conduct and measures to ensure that diversity is reflected among staff were among the measures recommended by the Programme of Action adopted by the 2001 World Conference Against Racism, Racial Discrimination,

Xenophobia and Related Intolerance.[20] The European Union (EU), for its part, is currently considering a proposal by EU Justice Commissioner Franco Frattini to establish a voluntary code of conduct for media organizations to counter "the false attribution of certain values and practices of Islam."[21]

In Britain, an advertising campaign showing famous faces with a skin color different from their actual one and asking viewers questions such as "Would I be less scary?" (in the case of former Spice Girls member Scary Spice shown with lighter skin) has "received massive print coverage" and inspired "numerous talk shows, panel discussions and radio call-ins." It has also been well received by ethnic minority newspapers and magazines.[22]

The British Council Austria and the International Organization for Migration have produced a "Resource Pack for Journalists Reporting on Migration," which was launched in April 2006.[23] This online tool "offers media experts access to a large network of journalists and organisations, a glossary on migration related topics, tips for appropriate use of images, tips for the sensitive use of language, [and] a collection of useful links."[24]

Within the EU, the EU Monitoring Centre on Racism and Xenophobia runs several initiatives on media and xenophobia. It commissioned a voluminous, comprehensive and very valuable report entitled "Racism and Cultural Diversity in European Media. An overview of research and good practice in the EU Members States, 1995-2000," published by the European Research Centre on Migration and Ethnic Relations (ERCOMER) in 2002.[25] The European Union Crisis Management (EUCM) recently organized a seminar for journalists and media practitioners from Europe, North Africa and the Middle East on the influence of media on intercultural relations and racism, which recommended, *inter alia*, better representation of minorities in newsrooms through targeted training and recruitment, more diversity in mainstream and non-fiction programs, making training in intercultural understanding a standard component of journalist education, and improved self-regulation and self-initiatives that promote ethical standards in reporting.[26] The Council of Europe's Parliamentary Assembly announced in March 2006 that it is "preparing a report on the image of asylum-seekers, migrants and refugees in the media."[27]

As far as the relationship between hate speech, communal conflict and genocide is concerned, many international donors and non-governmental organizations have supported and even run so-called peace radios and community radios advocating harmonious community relations. However, these efforts have so far focused mainly on post-conflict phases and/or have been linked to peacekeeping missions.[28] There have been very few initiatives where radio stations advocating peace have been supported specifically as a preventive measure in situations where communal conflict was ripe but had not yet erupted.[29] The United Nations (UN) Committee on the Elimination of Racial Discrimination recently published a list of "indicators of patterns of systematic and massive discrimination," among which are "[g]rossly biased versions of historical events in school textbooks and other educational materials as well as celebrations of historical events that exacerbate tensions between groups and peoples" and "[s]ystematic and widespread use and acceptance of speech and propaganda promoting hatred and/or inciting violence against minority groups, particularly in the media."[30]

The following are among the main strategies that have been used and promoted for combating hate on the Internet: legislation; self-regulation by the Internet industry, including through the adoption of codes of conduct; education of users through subscriber policies, codes of conduct, or educational websites; blocking and filtering software; rating and labeling systems; hotlines for users to alert police or Internet service providers; and active partnerships between Internet service providers and national governments.[31] However, each of these approaches is not without problems. For example, filtering software can be over-inclusive, rating systems are a massive challenge given the number of websites in existence, voluntary codes of conduct will never cover all service providers, and hate sites are likely to be moved to providers that have not adopted such codes, etc. Legislation against hate sites exists on a national basis, but there are states that oppose such legislation on the grounds that it violates freedom of speech.[32] The United States (US) is the best-known advocate of this position, but not the only one. The European Commission proposed a draft for an EU framework decision on combating racism and xenophobia in 2001,[33] but when the Council of Ministers last discussed the topic in July 2005, agreement could still not be reached because of differing views on the compatibility of such a decision with freedom of the press.[34]

3. Dilemmas

There are two basic dilemmas related to the issue of xenophobia and media stereotyping. First, the media can disseminate hatred, xenophobia, prejudice, negative stereotypes, etc., but they can also teach people about other cultures and provide information to overcome stereotypes and xenophobia. The dilemma is in ensuring that it does the second but not the first. The second dilemma is related to the two basic legal norms relevant to the issue of xenophobia in the media: freedom of the press and the prohibition of the dissemination of racism and racial hatred. There is a long-standing debate over the degree to which they are compatible and, where they are not, which takes precedence.[35] In the United States, freedom of speech is given extensive protection under the First Amendment to the Constitution. In Europe, freedom of speech is also protected, but most countries have legislation curtailing that right with a prohibition against the incitement of racial hatred. Thus, the second dilemma is in trying to ensure that freedom of speech is protected while also guaranteeing that the media have a positive influence on society. A further challenge is to ensure that measures taken to prevent xenophobia in the media are not used as a pretext for restricting freedom of speech in other areas not related to xenophobia and negative stereotyping.

Journalists covering minority- or migrant-related stories sometimes face a more specific dilemma, as they may find their stories relegated to less-visible parts of the newspaper or radio or television program that they are working for, and they may risk being labeled as someone interested in soft news stories that do not sell. This means that viewers, listeners, and readers who are most responsive to xenophobic stereotyping, and who could thus benefit most from these journalists' stories, are not easily exposed to them. Journalists in these situations face the dilemma of either adapting their style and even the content of their reporting in order to be able to have maximum impact on the public and maximum influence within their media outlet or staying true to their style and favorite topics but being allocated work that will mostly be noticed only by the "converted."[36]

4. Implications

In the absence of a consensus on how to reconcile the prohibition of incitement to racism and xenophobia and the freedom of speech, and given that journalists cannot be forced to write a certain way, measures to combat xenophobia and stereotyping have to be addressed differently.

Apart from trying to influence the supply side, i.e., media output, by convincing journalists and media outlets of the usefulness and benefits of addressing minority issues in a fair way, emphasis has to be laid on educating the public on how to use the media, i.e., on improving its media literacy.

5. Future Trajectories/Scenarios

As media reporting and political agendas are intrinsically linked and influence one another, it is difficult to predict scenarios for the future of xenophobia and stereotyping in the media and their role in global insecurity. As the row over the cartoons of the Prophet Mohammed in a Danish newspaper has shown, the issue of press freedom and the responsibilities it entails is extremely controversial today. Events such as the printing of the cartoons in Denmark provide an opportunity for an in-depth debate about what freedom of speech means, where it ends, what it entails in terms of responsibility, and, importantly, about the fact that every culture, society, and individual, consciously or unconsciously, respects certain taboos and thus voluntarily imposes limits on its freedom of speech. There has so far not been such a debate in the wider public except for a very short period of time just after the uproar over the cartoons, and it does not seem likely to take place in the near future.[37]

As to the portrayal of immigrants, asylum seekers, and refugees in the media, a major change will not take place unless European political leaders decide to replace the current debate on security and policies focusing on keeping immigrants out at all costs to a debate that highlights respect and understanding for the reasons why immigrants choose to come to Europe and the benefits of immigration and policies that show acceptance of Europe as a continent of immigration. As mentioned, the media can to a certain extent influence the political agenda, but the media cannot by itself change European immigration policies and the discourses of political leaders, even if many more journalists and media outlets were committed to correcting the distorting images of immigrants that most of them currently portray. Rather, in the context of the war on terrorism, it is likely that the discourse on immigration in the context of security will continue with even more vigor. On the other hand, recent demonstrations in the US in favor of immigration indicate an acknowledgement of the important economic role played by immigrants, and a positive stance on immigration on these grounds, by large parts of the population in that country at least.

6. Policy Recommendations

Peace radios to counter hate radios
UN, donors: Peace radios should also be used as a preventive tool. Donors: Increase reliable funding and long-term support and sustainable strategies for peace radios. Academia, NGOs: Research should be conducted on the effect of peace radios on intercommunal images and relations. The UN Peacebuilding Commission should include media monitoring in its activities for early detection of hate speech and texts, and should in this regard take into account the research mentioned above about recurring messages in hate speech.

Counter xenophobia and teach about stereotypes in primary education and beyond
School curricula have to be updated to include education about the origins and nature of racism, xenophobia, and other forms of discrimination. This should be based on the notion that there is but one human race and should include facilitation of personal contacts with minority groups. History curricula and textbooks should also, where necessary, be updated or entirely rewritten to eliminate portrayals of one nation or country as being infallible and to reflect the fact that historical accounts are always human-made and subjective. In cases of recent armed conflict, history textbooks should be written jointly by historians from all parties involved in the conflict. A good example of this is a group of 60 historians from 11 countries in the Balkans who are currently producing history materials for teachers in secondary schools in this region. These teaching materials aim to introduce students to "multiperspectiveness," i.e. the views of different states and the fact that societies are always divided on different historical events. The Serbian editions of these new books have just been published and other language editions will follow.[38] Media-literacy education should be included in all school curricula and should teach pupils how to detect stereotypes.

Give minorities' voices more space in newspapers and broadcasts
Tabloid newspapers should consider publishing editorials by members of minority groups so that they can give an account of their daily lives. This would allow readers to get an entirely different view of the life of, and problems encountered by, minorities, in a style that attracts readers of tabloids more than long background reports would. TV and radio programs featuring minorities in non-stereotypical roles should be given prime-time slots. Editors should be lobbied to recognize the importance of minority audiences.

Make existing handbooks and guidelines much more widely available to journalists working in all genres
There exists a multitude of handbooks and guidelines on reporting diversity and avoiding stereotypes, but they should be much more accessible to journalists who are not actively involved in minority projects or whose media outlets do not have their own guidelines.

Use innovative advertising campaigns to raise awareness about racism and xenophobia
The example of the British anti-racism advertising campaign mentioned above shows that such campaigns reach a wide part of the population and can spark animated debate among it. Another example is a public discussion where a speaker replaced the word Gypsy in newspaper headlines with terms such as Jew, black, or Muslim, and thus raised awareness of the racist language used. This could be adapted for an advertising campaign.[39]

Help minority organizations establish effective, professional media strategies
Minority organizations should be given financial and other support to establish media strategies that allow them to be effective partners for media outlets looking for information about minorities and for those looking for minority representatives for interviews, etc. Minority organizations should, *inter alia*, be able to provide media with sources, images, information on terminology and pitfalls in reporting, background, and contextualization of statistics. They should be trained to organize professional media conferences and publish professional press releases.[40] More training should also be given to minority journalists to help them enter mainstream journalism if they so wish.

Authorities should review their policies on the publication of statistics on crime, minorities, and immigration

Authorities should be made aware of the misinterpretations and ensuing discrimination that can result from the way statistics on crime, minorities, or immigration are presented. In particular, they need to be convinced to provide more context and background when publishing figures, such as comparisons with other, extra-European countries, or information on those asylum seekers who were judged to fulfill the criteria to be granted asylum, not just on those who were not.[41]

Media councils should deal with xenophobia, racism, and related discrimination by the media

Media councils should promote dialogue and establish guidelines on how to report on minorities and what constitutes unacceptable reporting. Based on this, they should accept complaints against xenophobia, racism, stereotyping, and related discrimination by the media.[42]

References

---

[1] Merriam-Webster Online Dictionary, http://www.m-w.com/cgi-bin/dictionary.

[2] J.T. Wal, "Racism and Cultural Diversity in European Media: A Review of Research," paper presented at the National Conference of the Federal Commission against Racism, "Parler non pas de, mais avec les minorities – Le racisme et les minorities dans les medias," University of Bern, March 21, 2003.

[3] *Ibid.*

[4] This subtle form of racism evident in the reporting by European media on issues of immigration is called "essentialism:" "Essentialism means that actions or attitudes of for example a (group of) Muslim(s) in the news are not only generalised to the whole Muslim community, but also that their features are represented as unchangeable innate features, which inextricably belong to and have and will always belong to that group." *Ibid.*

[5] "What's the story? Results From Research Into Media Coverage of Refugees and Asylum Seekers in the UK," *Article XIX*, November 2003, see http://www.article19.org/pdfs/publications/refugees-what-s-the-story-.pdf.

[6] The most popular themes across three very different newspapers were found to be exclusion policies aimed at "bogus" asylum applicants, crime/terrorism perpetrated by asylum seekers, and accommodation/detention of applicants awaiting decisions. See M. Randall, "Comparing the Daily Telegraph, The Guardian and The Independent, Guest Media Lens Alert: Asylum and Immigration," December 8, 2003, available at http://www.medialens.org/alerts/03/031208_Asylum_Immigration.HTM.

[7] See L. Bishop, *Anti-Nicaraguan Xenophobia and Newspaper Editorial Policy in Costa Rica: Analysis and Suggestions* (Chicago: University of Chicago Press, 2001).

[8] R. Danso and D.A. McDonald, "Writing Xenophobia: Immigration and the Print Media in Post-apartheid South Africa," *Africa Today*, Vol. 48, Issue 3, Fall 2001, pp. 115-137, from abstract.

[9] "Racism, racial discrimination and related intolerance relating to the media, including new information technologies," background paper prepared by Bent Sørensen at the OHCHR/UNESCO Workshop to Develop a Publication to Combat Racism and to Foster

Tolerance, Implementation of the Programme of Action of the Third Decade to Combat Racism and Racial Discrimination, Paris, February 19-20, 2003, December 26, 2002, HR/PARIS/SEM.3/2003/BP.9.

[10] Report by the Canadian Human Rights Foundation, quoted in "Racism, Racial Discrimination, Xenophobia and All Forms of Discrimination. Situation of Muslim and Arab peoples in various parts of the world in the aftermath of the events of 11 September 2001," report by D. Diène, special rapporteur on contemporary forms of racism, racial discrimination, xenophobia and related intolerance, submitted pursuant to Commission on Human Rights Resolution 2002/9, January 3, 2003, E/CN.4/2003/23. See also C. Allen and J.S. Nielsen, "Summary Report on Islamophobia in the EU after 11 September 2001," European Monitoring Centre on Racism and Xenophobia, Vienna, May 2002. For a general discussion of media after September 11, 2001, see B. Hayes and A White, Journalism, "Civil Liberties and the War on Terrorism: A Special Report by the International Federation of Journalists and Statewatch," 2005, and International Council on Human Rights Policy, "Human Rights after September 11," 2002, pp. 38-41.

[11] "The Impact of 7 July 2005 London Bomb Attacks on Muslim Communities in the EU," European Monitoring Centre on Racism and Xenophobia, November 2005.

[12] Quoted in M. Maneria and J.T. Wal, "The Criminalisation of Ethnic Groups: An Issue for Media Analysis," *Forum: Qualitative Social Research*, Vol. 6, No. 3, Art. 9, September 2005.

[13] F.D. Gilliam, Jr., and S. Iyengar, "Prime Suspects: The Influence of Local Television News on the Viewing Public," *American Journal of Political Science*, Vol. 44, No. 3, July 2000, p. 571.

[14] "Serb TV started with a steady flow of negative comments on other republics, with frequent interviews of Serb nationalists, before moving on to a more robust campaign aimed at raising fears of Croatia by showing footage of the Jasenovac concentration camp run by Croat Nazi sympathizers during World War II. This was aimed at gathering support for the Serb cause during the Serbs' rebellion in Krajina (...). In 1990 Serb TV led a campaign against ethnic Albanians in Kosovo, accusing them of 'poisoning wells and slitting the throats of children.'" M. Fachot, "Survey of 'hate' and 'humanitarian' broadcast media operating in zones of conflict," Fondation Hirondelle, Survey prepared originally in 1998, most recent update in April, 2000, see http://www.hirondelle.org/hirondelle.nsf/0/c584cdc24a63e9e6c12568e4005f1463?OpenDocument. On the danger of unintentional fueling of inter-communal violence by media reporting and the media's responsibility in war reporting, see J. Bransten, "Kosovo: Violence Raises Questions About Media Responsibility," Radio Free Europe/Radio Liberty, March 19, 2004, available at http://www.rferl.org/featuresarticle/2004/03/034b7105-9d90-4b91-b9b3-7dfadd724614.html.

[15] J. Snyder and K. Ballentine, "Nationalism and the Marketplace of Ideas," *International Security*, Vol. 21, No. 2, Fall 1996.

[16] Caslon Analytics, e-politics and democracy guide, available at http://www.caslon.com.au/politicsguide6.htm and Sørensen, *op. cit.*, note 9. The former also contains a good general overview and discussion of the nature, prevalence and responses to hate sites.

[17] On the relationship between hate sites and hate crimes, see "OSCE Meeting on the Relationship between Racis, Xenophobic and Anti-Semitic Propaganda on the Internet and Hate Crimes," Paris, June 16-17, 2004, consolidated summary, OSCE Document PC.DEL/918/04/ Corr.1, September 27, 2004, and International Network against Cybercrime, Hate on the Net. Virtual nursery for In Real Life crime, June 2004, available at http://www.inach.net/content/inach-hateonthenet.pdf.

[18] See the network's website for more information on its projects and for further resources: http://www.olmcm.org. See also the following paper by the IFJ, written in 1997, but whose content remains valid to a large extent: International Federation of Journalists (IFJ), "Media and Tolerance. Background Paper," UN/UNESCO European Seminar on Promoting Independent and Pluralistic Media Sofia, Bulgaria, September 10-13, 1997, available at http://unesdoc.unesco.org/images/0011/001117/111758eo.pdf.

[19] International Federation of Journalists (IFJ) Declaration of Principles on the Conduct of Journalists, Adopted by 1954 World Congress of the IFJ. Amended by the 1986 World Congress, available at http://www.ifj.org/default.asp?Issue=ETHICS&Language=EN.

[20] The Declaration and Programme of Action of the 2001 World Conference Against Racism, Racial Discrimination, Xenophobia and Related Intolerance is contained in the following United Nations General Assembly document: A/CONF.189/12, "Report of the World Conference against Racism, Racial Discrimination, Xenophobia and Related Intolerance Durban," August 31 - September 8, 2001, January 25, 2002, available at http://www.unhchr.ch/huridocda/huridoca.nsf/(Symbol)/A.Conf.189.12.En?Opendocument. The Declaration and Programme of Action are also available at http://www.unhchr.ch/pdf/Durban.pdf.

[21] B. Waterfield, "EU media code to follow Muslim cartoon row," EUPolitix.com, February 3, 2006.

[22] "An Innovative Media Partnership against Racism, Durban 2001 – United against Racism," *Newsletter of the World Conference against Racism Secretariat*, Issue 2, February 2001.

[23] On September 26-27, 2005, the British Council Austria and the International Organization for Migration organized a seminar entitled "Media and Migration – Through the Eyes of the Other." General Recommendations for a "Resource Pack for Journalists Reporting on Migration" were developed during this seminar. The Resource Pack was launched during a conference convoked by the Austrian Presidency of the EU on Media, Migration and Asylum on April 19, 2006 in Vienna and is available at http://www.emn.at/media/index.php?module=Content&func=main&idc=1&newlang=eng.

[24] The Britsh Council, "Launch of Online Tool for Journalists," http://www.britishcouncil.org/austria-whats-on-media-resource-pack.htm.

[25] J.T. Wal, (ed.), "Racism and Cultural Diversity in European Media. An overview of research and good practice in the EU Members States, 1995-2000 on behalf of the European Monitoring Centre on Racism and Xenophobia, Vienna (EUMC)" by European Research Centre on Migration and Ethnic Relations (ERCOMER), Vienna, February 2002.

[26] The conference was entitled "Racism, Xenophobia and the Media: Towards respect and understanding of all religions and cultures" and took place in Vienna on May 22 and 23. See EUMC Bulletin 2/2006, "Journalists discuss racism in the media at EUMC media seminar," http://www.eumc.europa.eu/eumc/index.php?fuseaction=content.dsp_cat_content&catid=4434e55adcab7.

[27] Parliamentary Assembly of the Council of Europe, Council of Europe parliamentarians call for "a constant vigil against discrimination, hate speech and stereotyping in the media," press release, Brussels, March 21, 2006, http://assembly.coe.int/ASP/Press/StopPressView.asp?CPID=1742. In 1995, the same body had issued its Recommendation 1277 on migrants, ethnic minorities and media. For further action by the Council of Europe (CoE) in this field, see the Political Declaration and the three Resolutions adopted by the CoE's 7th European Ministerial Conference on Mass Media Policy, "Integration and Diversity: the New Frontiers of European Media and Communications Policy," Kyiv, March 10-11, 2005. UNESCO, for its part, also adopted a declaration on the issue: Declaration on Promoting Independent and Pluralistic Media (Declaration of Sofia), adopted in Sofia, September 13, 1997 and endorsed by the 29th UNESCO General Conference, Paris, 21 October to November 12, 1997.

[28] For an example of a "peace radio" set up and run by a UN peacekeeping mission, see two recent articles in the UN Chronicle Online Edition (Issue 6, 2006): "United Nations Operation in Côte d'Ivoire (UNOCI), UN's Efforts to Counter Hate Media in Côte d'Ivoire," available at http://www.un.org/Pubs/chronicle/2006/issue3/0306p36b.htm and P. Witcher, "Hate Media: Gagging Côte d'Ivoire's Peace Process," available at http://www.un.org/Pubs/chronicle/2006/issue3/0306p36.htm.

[29] Fachot, *op. cit.*, note 14. For another measure to curb hate radios' success, see J.F. Metzl, "Information Intervention: When Switching Channels Isn't Enough," *Foreign Affairs*, Nov/Dec 1997, Vol. 76, Issue 6, pp.15-20.

[30] Committee on the Elimination of Racial Discrimination, "Decision to follow up on the declaration on the prevention of genocide: indicators of patterns of systematic and massive racial discrimination," October 14, 2005, CERD/C/67/1.

[31] M. Shaw and O. Barchechat, "Preventing Hate Crimes: International Strategies and Practice,"

International Centre for the Prevention of Crime, April 2002, p. 25; United Nations General Assembly document A/CONF.189/PC.2/12, "Review of Reports, Studies and Other Documentation for the Preparatory Committee and the World Conference, Report of the High Commissioner for Human Rights on the use of the Internet for purposes of incitement of racial hatred, racist propaganda and xenophobia, and on ways of promoting international cooperation in this area," report submitted to the Preparatory Committee of the World Conference Against Racism, Racial Discrimination, Xenophobia and Related Intolerance, April 27, 2001.

[32] On an international basis, there is the Council of Europe's Additional Protocol to the convention on Cybercrime concerning the criminalization of acts of a racist and xenophobic nature committed through computer systems, adopted on November 7, 2002 and which entered into force on March 1, 2006. To date, nine states have ratified the Additional Protocol.

[33] Commission of the European Communities, "Proposal for a Council Framework Decision on combating racism and xenophobia," Brussels, November 28, 2001, COM(2001) 664 final, 2001/0270 (CNS).

[34] Luxembourg Presidency of the Council of the European Union, "No agreement on the framework decision on combating racism and xenophobia at the Justice and Home Affairs Council," Press Release, June 2, 2005, available at http://www.eu2005.lu/en/actualites/communiques/2005/06/02jai-rx/index.html.

[35] Several international treaties establish the relevant basic norms of international law applicable to the issue of xenophobia in the media: International Covenant on Civil and Political Rights, International Convention on the Elimination of All Forms of Racial Discrimination, European Convention for the Protection of Human Rights and Fundamental Freedoms. Also see the following declarations for further international norms: UNESCO Declaration on Race and Racial Prejudice (1978), Media Experts Commission of the OSCE, Council of Europe's 1993 Vienna Declaration, Declaration on Media in a Democratic Society adopted by the 4th Council of Europe Ministerial Conference on Mass Media Policy, Prague 1994.

[36] C. Cortés, "A Long Way to Go: Minorities and the Media," *Media and Values*, Issue 38, Winter 1987: "Minority journalists often face [the] dilemma of balancing their social commitment to provide better coverage of minority communities against their fears of being 'ghettoized' to the 'minority beat' and thereby having their professional careers restricted."

[37] The EUMC did contribute to such a public debate by dedicating the entire June 2006 issue of its Magazine *Equal Voices* to the topic of freedom of speech and hate speech. The issue, entitled "The Right to offend and the right not to be offended," is available online at http://eumc.europa.eu/eumc/material/pub/ev/ev18/ev-18.pdf.

[38] S. Dubravka, "Historians Are Not Judges," Helsinki Charter, No. 89-90, November/December 2005. See also the South-East Europe Textbook Network at http://www.ffzg.hr/seetn/ and F.I. Toloudi, "The Image of the 'Other'/the Neighbor in the School Textbooks of the Balkan Countries," Macedonian Heritage, December 1, 1998, available at http://www.macedonian-heritage.gr/Contributions/contr_Toludi1198.html.

[39] M. Pesic, "Media vs. Discrimination and Xenophobia," in "The Role of Media and Politics in Fighting Racism, Xenophobia and Discrimination, Seminar Reader," issued for a seminar of the same title organised by the International Federation of Liberal Youth, November 18-24, 2005, Skopje, Macedonia, compiled by K.P. Jené, International Federation of Liberal Youth.

[40] See C. Thompson, "Migration and the media," Migration Policy Group, EMP Issue Paper 2, prepared for the European Migration Dialogue, October 2005, and J.T. Wal and E. Lubanau, "On Line/More Colour in the Media: NGO's need more training in media work," *EUMC Equal Voices*, Issue 9.

[41] Article XIX, *op. cit.*, note 5.

[42] *Ibid.*, and Jené, *op. cit.*, note 39.

CHAPTER 5

EDITORIAL OF POLICY BRIEF ON XENOPHOBIA, MEDIA STEREOTYPING, AND THEIR ROLE IN GLOBAL INSECURITY

NAYEF R.F. AL-RODHAN

Dr. Nayef R.F. Al-Rodhan is Senior Scholar in Geostrategy and Director of the Program on the Geopolitical Implications of Globalization and Transnational Security at the Geneva Centre for Security Policy, Geneva, Switzerland

1. Review and Critique

As Jan Aart Scholte has commented, "The more that distance and borders have disintegrated, the more national differences have seemed precious."[1] Faced with increased migration and economic uncertainty within a globalizing economy, intolerance of non-citizens and refugees, as well as of minorities, can sometimes be pervasive as people seek to stave off perceived dangers to their national identity. In the worst-case scenario, this can lead to abuse of migrants, refugees, and ethnic minorities. Perceived as a cause, as well as a symptom, of many such risks, globalization seems to have prompted nationalists to rally to the defense of the cherished values that are perceived as being under siege. Cris Shore even goes so far as to state that, "[l]ike decapitating the mythical hydra, the break-up of old nation-states may simply replace them with a plethora of new nationalisms often more xenophobic and ethnically exclusivist than that from which they seceded."[2]

The defense of national groups against the perceived threats of "others" is a significant source of insecurity for many. The media is central to this process of "other-ing." Bo Petersson describes images as "cognitive and affective conceptual lenses, organizing devices and information filters." These images, as Petersson notes, are socially constructed. To this end, they can be confirmed or reconstructed. Images of people may become entrenched or they be malleable, changing either in a positive or negative direction, depending on how we filter and interpret information.[3] Most stereotypes are formed on the basis of little first-hand knowledge and are often based on hearsay. This implies that negative images have very little opportunity of being deconstructed and reconstructed in a more positive light.

Exposure to stereotyping in the media influences the way that people view the groups being represented. As Katja Flückiger explains in her brief, Muslims, Sinti and Roma (often referred to as "gypsies") are often represented as constituting a threat to the security of more established populations.[4] They tend to be portrayed as sinister and often as the perpetrators of crime. In fact, the discourse on immigrant groups, as well as on refugees, is often framed almost solely in terms of their profiting from welfare systems and criminality. Images of these groups as an enemy may lead members of a national group, for example, to take pre-emptory action against what they perceive as a growing threat. Those that are the victims of stereotyping may find themselves the target of suspicion and aggression. If the media does nothing to contradict negative stereotypes, they are likely to serve to feed xenophobia and to legitimize populist policies.[5]

As Flückiger argues, the role of the media in nurturing either negative or positive images of people other than the established population must be taken into account by journalists and their representative bodies. Indeed, a number of measures have been taken by media organizations, states, international organizations, and migrant organizations in an effort to reduce xenophobic stereotyping in the media. Yet, initiatives aimed at curbing xenophobic stereotyping are confronted with the dilemma of doing so without curtailing freedom of speech and expression.

2. Dilemmas and Our Recommendations

The policy challenges posed by the role of the media in either promoting negative or positive images of people are primarily associated with encouraging the media to take steps to curtail xenophobic stereotyping, while at the same time preserving freedom of speech. We suggest eight dilemmas or challenges facing policy makers, as well as eight corresponding recommendations.

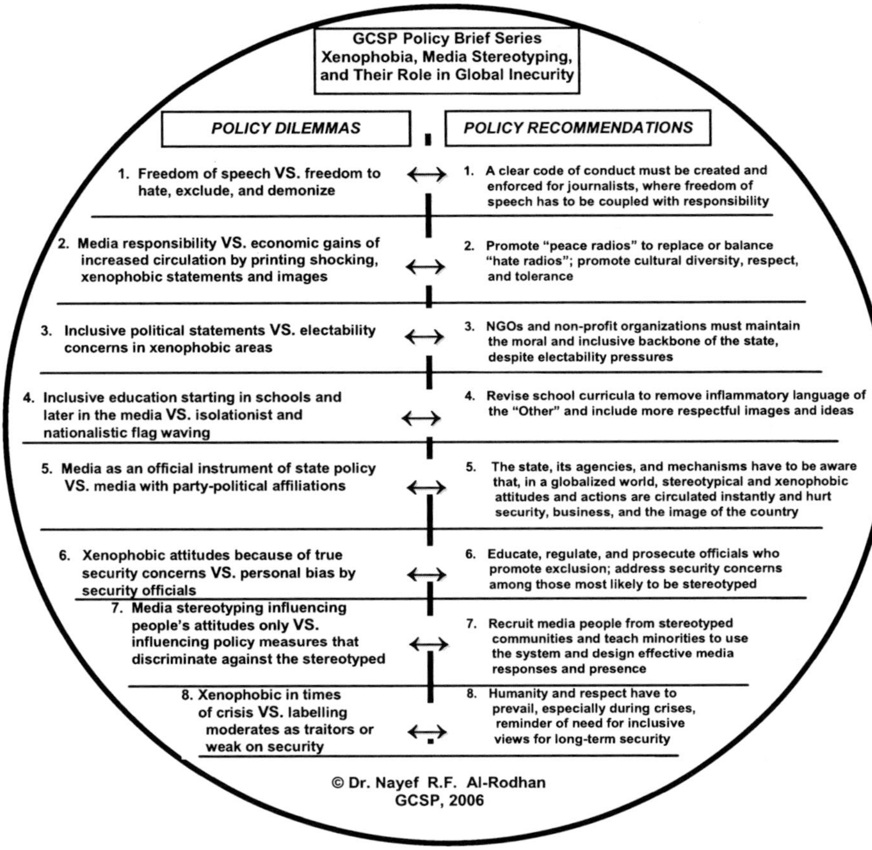

The principal dilemma related to responding appropriately to xenophobic stereotyping is limiting the freedom to hate, demonize, and exclude without curbing freedom of speech. We suggest that a clear code of conduct for journalists should be created and enforced, coupling freedom of speech with responsibility.

Some commentators argue that xenophobic stereotyping simply reflects dominant views within societies. This being the case, it represents a considerable challenge. Media responsibility effectively competes with the economic gains of increased circulation as a result of printing shocking, xenophobic statements or images. Ultimately, underlying prejudices within societies need to be confronted and changed. Long-term measures should be taken to promote more inclusive societies. In order to balance "hate radios," for example, "peace radios" should be promoted, along with cultural diversity, respect, and tolerance.

Another balance that needs to be struck is between making the media an official instrument of state policy or an entity with specific political-party affiliations. Both of these extremes render the media incapable of serving the people effectively. The state, its agencies, and mechanisms have to be aware that, in a globalized world, stereotypical and xenophobic attitudes and actions are circulated instantly and hurt security, business, and the image of the country.

Xenophobic sentiments may increase in times of crisis. This has been perceptible in many countries in relation to immigration and asylum seekers, as well as international terrorism, for example. In such instances, moderates who speak out against this may be labeled as either traitors or weak on security. Yet, humanity and respect must prevail, especially during times of crisis. We need to be reminded of the need for inclusivity as an investment in long-term security. Xenophobia and racism are only likely to generate alienation and frustration, which can only lead to further problems of security and stability.

An additional challenge is to distinguish between xenophobic attitudes related to true security concerns and those generated from the personal bias of security officials. While both are equally reprehensible and ought to be minimized, the latter should be treated separately. Officials who promote exclusion should be educated, regulated, and prosecuted. The security concerns of those most likely to be stereotyped should also be addressed.

The problem is that media stereotyping influences not only people's attitudes but also policies that discriminate against the stereotyped. One way to address this issue is to better represent the cultural diversity of societies in the media establishment itself. Journalists and those working in media organizations ought to be recruited from stereotyped communities. Minorities should also be encouraged and taught how to use the system and to design effective media responses and presence.

3. Conclusion

Xenophobic media stereotyping should be taken seriously, since it increases insecurity among targeted groups. This can lead to discriminatory policies, tension, and even physical violence and genocide. A decrease in opportunities for xenophobic stereotyping needs to be accompanied by long-term educational measures that encourage tolerance and inclusivity within societies, even during times of crisis.

References

[1] J.A. Scholte, *Globalization: A Critical Introduction* (Houndmills: Palgrave, 2000), p. 226.
[2] C. Shore, *Building Europe: The Cultural Politics of European Integration* (London: Routledge, 2000), p. 232.
[3] B. Petersson, "Combating Uncertainty, Combating the Global: Scapegoating, Xenophobia and the National-Local Nexus," accessed at http://ask.lub.lu.se/archive/00026066/01/Petersson.htm, p. 3.
[4] For the brief in its entirety, please see Chapter 4.
[5] Petersson, *op. cit.*, note 3.

CHAPTER 6

DANISH CARTOONS: A SYMPTOM OF GLOBAL INSECURITY

GRAEME HERD
NAYEF R.F. AL-RODHAN

Dr. Graeme Herd is Joint Course Director of the International Training Course in Security Policy at the Geneva Centre for Security Policy, Geneva, Switzerland

Dr. Nayef R.F. Al-Rodhan is Senior Scholar in Geostrategy and Director of the Program on the Geopolitical Implications of Globalization and Transnational Security at the Geneva Centre for Security Policy, Geneva, Switzerland

Abstract
The Danish cartoon controversy reflects rising resentment and a challenge not to the mobility of Euro-Atlantic goods and commodities but to the region's dominant cultural norms and values. The resonance of the reaction to the publication, particularly in the Middle East, shocked the Danish political elite and public, and the cartoon controversy represented, for some, the worst foreign policy disaster since the Second World War. The backlash to the controversy damaged Denmark's reputation in the Middle East; stigmatized its diplomatic efforts, and so its effectiveness as an internationalist political actor; and raised questions about the durability and place of its core identity and values in an ever more interconnected world. As an event, however, it may have facilitated the creation, albeit unplanned, of a global civil society.

1. Policy Challenges

The Danish cartoon controversy provides an unusual example of cultural globalization, where it has been possible to track the origin, measure the flow, and gauge the effect of an idea. On September 30, 2005, the Danish newspaper *Jyllandes-Posten* published 12 cartoons that satirized the Prophet Mohammed as, for example, a cleric wearing a bomb for a turban. By February 2006, after a four-month interval, promoters of Muslim discontent organized propaganda campaigns in

Europe and the Middle East, and the international press reported attacks on the Danish and Norwegian embassies in Damascus; mobs in Tehran, Cairo, and Beirut; protests in London, Paris, and Copenhagen; and the deaths of 11 people in related violence in Afghanistan.

The violent response to the cartoons caused a number of policy challenges for Western liberal democratic and secular governments. For example, they were forced to consider whether the freedoms of thought and expression were unconditional or whether they could be limited, as well as the relationship between those freedoms and the responsibility not to incite hatred. In addition, governments were forced to consider their relations with the Muslim world, including ways to bridge growing divides in terms of values, religion, and culture.

2. Responses

The cartoon issue has fuelled Islamophobia in Europe and helped reinforce and authenticate extremist narratives in both Europe and the Middle East that reflect atavistic binary thinking and that divide, rather than unite, societies. Some have argued that Western newspapers printed the cartoons to boost their circulation rather than to show support for freedom of expression; that freedom of expression does not mean freedom to be insensitive, unnecessarily gratuitous, or hostile to the growing diversity within Western societies. For others, the protests were a *coup de theatre* intended to achieve a secular political result, as *agents provocateurs* circulated the cartoons widely to incite riots.

In Denmark, the issue helped polarize society, as it occurred in the context of an ongoing debate over immigration and amid a rise in extreme right-wing parties. Kamal Qureshi, a member of the Danish Socialist People's Party, argued: “The cartoons were the symbol of a very xenophobic agenda that has been going on which is led by the Danish People’s Party, which is a radical, racist party in the Danish parliament.” He noted: “It’s very important to know why this happened in Denmark, and why this didn't happen in some other country.... The approach in Norway and Sweden towards the ethnic minorities has been completely different. Sweden created a mosque many, many years ago in one of the biggest cities. In Denmark there is still to be built a mosque where the Muslims can go and have their prayers."[1] The role of a hitherto durable dominant political culture based on political anti-elitism and egalitarianism was challenged by these events, leading to a greater questioning of hidden assumptions concerning the nature of Danish identity and self-image.

3. Dilemmas

Situations that require a choice between two alternatives that are or appear to be equally unfavorable or mutually exclusive place states and their policy makers "between the devil and the deep blue sea." When we reflect on the issues addressed in this policy brief, it becomes apparent that the classical security dilemma, first coined by John Herz in 1950, needs to be reconsidered when states and non-state actors occupy and are increasingly at cross purposes within a globalized world. According to Herz, a security dilemma occurs where the security of one state requires or leads to the insecurity of another. However, the Danish cartoon controversy demonstrated that, as the scale and intensity of globalization increases, the appropriate functioning of non-state actors (an independent newspaper) within a state (Denmark) can result in challenges by external non-state actors (mobilized public opinion in the Middle East) leading to symbolic and actual undermining of state security (Danish Embassy attacked and economic boycott of Danish goods). This might be termed a state/non-state security dilemma.

1. States should protect the fundamental freedoms of their populations, but when connectivity causes local actions to have a global impact, and states are punished over actions they are not responsible for and are unable to respond to without changing the nature of their governance, how can states respond meaningfully while maintaining their integrity?

2. The right to provoke and freedom of expression are key tenets of liberal democratic states, as are the responsibility to respect the views of others and not to incite hatred or violence. But favoring one side of this balance weakens the other, which raises the question of where to draw the line without damaging both.

3. How can homogeneous states (where there is one dominant ethnicity, religion, and value base) best maintain the core identity of the societies within it while integrating ever more closely into a globalized world where identities and values can clash?

4. Those states and communities that can access and adapt new technologies gain the benefits of globalization, but, at the same time, the greater the connectivity offered by information and communication technologies, the sharper and more immediate the clash in values, ethics, and religions between communities, the greater the resulting instability, and the more globalization is undermined. How can this be managed, and can an equilibrium be found when low- and high-context cultures inevitably clash?[2]

4. Implications

The foreign policy implications of the cartoon controversy placed a spotlight on the extent to which the freedom of the press and speech can infringe on a discourse of tolerance and respect. It raised a number of questions that are unresolved in democratic states and societies: How are the two to be balanced – should individuals and communities be willing to tolerate insults, mockery, and ridicule? Who decides? What is the role of religion and religious sensitivities in a secular and democratic state? How can minorities that do not share the same ethnicity, language, or religion best be integrated?

The constructed self-image of the Danish nation, whose core identity is based on an ethnically and culturally homogeneous imagined community, was challenged as the growth (5.4 percent of the population), attitudes, and expectations of Muslim communities became much more visible within Denmark. This has important implications and has helped Denmark's identity evolve.

The cartoon episode also highlighted the way in which Danish, and to a lesser extent European, news media were increasingly prone to depict Muslims as radicals and terrorists. The media distorted the fact that 80 percent of Denmark's Muslims were drawn from countries like Turkey, Pakistan, Iran, and Somalia. They were not members of political or religious groups. Indeed, only 5 percent describe themselves as religious, although the "stigmatization of Muslims in this country risks turning the cliché of the radical Muslim into a reality."[3]

This stigmatization raised a more fundamental issue that has profound policy implications: how the relationship between Islam and culture is understood in the West. Islam provides a core part of a Muslim's identity, and so the reaction to the cartoons is explained by a reaction to an identity; however, not all Muslim responses were violent. The Muslim world is not monolithic, and a clear policy implication is to formulate policies that take into account how culture affects people's perception of the world and, in turn, helps determine their understanding of events. In the United States (US), for example, Muslim leaders shared the universal anger and outrage over the publication of the cartoons yet argued that the violence perpetrated by some Muslim communities and groups should stop because the Prophet Mohammed would never have approved. Presentation and perception matter as much as policies themselves.

This event has highlighted the way in which different globalization processes (economic, political, and cultural) are cross-cutting and intertwined, the way in which cultural and religious issues can have economic bearing, and the ways in which state and non-state actors can themselves be bound in a security dilemma: Globalization allowed communities to organize an economic boycott of goods from Denmark in retaliation for a perceived cultural/religious attack and provocation by a non-state actor over which the state had no control.

It also illustrated that publishing can no longer be considered local. The interaction of peoples from different cultural and religious worlds has broken the bounds of geography, and this requires a constant awareness of the interrelatedness of our world and the consequences of this for states, identities, and norms.

5. Future Trajectories/Scenarios

The concept of Denmark as a state within which lives a homogeneous nation can only be weakened and adapted as the free movement of labor within the European Union (EU) continues and as immigration into the EU increases. The question of the integration of minorities into Danish society (and indeed into Scandinavian societies more generally) will continue to be controversial, and higher unemployment, crime, and school dropout rates, as well as cultural isolation, will continue to testify to this fact.

The cartoon controversy made ordinary Muslims in Western Europe realize how rapidly perceptions about their role and place in society could deteriorate and how fragile and transitory their civic integration was. As one Muslim born in Africa and living in a major Western European city noted: "They think we are stupid, easily manipulated, and offended by trivial matters. And increasingly, we feel they do not want us around."[4] The nature of the challenge posed by the cartoons highlighted the fact that existing dialogue mechanisms between Western European governments and Muslims have failed and need to be replaced in order not to reinforce the current trajectory.

Denmark's commitments to securing stability in Afghanistan and Iraq are likely to come under much greater scrutiny by the people and parliaments in those countries. Thus, an attempt to clearly link such interventions to Danish security interests and strategy will have to be made. Over the longer term, active Danish internationalism in Middle East security politics will recover. However, its reputation has been damaged, and it will be much harder, for example, for Denmark to push democratization efforts in political governance as a result of its handling of this controversy, which can be utilized by conservative factions to demonstrate the destabilizing effect of democratization efforts. In particular, the Wider Middle East Initiative that was launched by the Danish government in 2003 will find less support.

The idea of a long-term evolution toward a global civil society has also been brought into question by the cartoon controversy, because it constituted and registered as a global event that caused a global reaction. In its aftermath, it has triggered a renewed emphasis on dialogue and understanding, the very lifeblood necessary for the formation of a global civil society. By forcing a debate on the issue, the cartoon controversy did have a constructive role: It highlighted the fact that people can have multiple identities (Muslim, democrat, Danish citizen) and underlined the importance of the values of tolerance, respect, and religious and cultural acceptance in a globalizing world. Though not universal, as an event it most likely facilitated the continued, albeit unplanned, construction of a global civil society: The integration of Muslim minorities into the mainstream has become a new national priority for many European countries. In addition, religious but peaceful activism in the Middle East in opposition to the cartoons can undercut the power and appeal of groups like Al-Qaida to recruit among disaffected youth on the grounds that only they are standard-bearers and defenders of their self-declared "true Islam." Such activism allows Muslims to act on behalf of their religion in a positive way and limits the attraction of extremist groups.

The ability of elites or non-state actors to capitalize on such controversies, indeed to publicize and disseminate images or messages in order to achieve their own local political objectives, will likely become more pronounced. But the greater the connectivity between societies, the greater the immunization of societies to such images and the less powerful their effect.

6. Policy Recommendations

States must implement awareness-raising campaigns to increase recognition among policy makers, politicians, the media, civil society, and the general public of the dilemmas associated with each aspect of globalization. Globalization carries with it the triggers that can cause a backlash against the processes it promotes. In particular, such campaigns should focus on the following:

1. The governments of democratic states should be quick to apologize for offenses caused to people's religious feelings but should not apologize on behalf of non-state actors that cause such offenses. Western states should engage in more thoughtful cultural diplomacy, explaining the realities and complexities of Western societies behind closed doors and openly where appropriate.[5]

2. Governments should encourage the media in their countries to correlate freedom of expression with responsibility and cultural sensitivity.

3. Governments on all sides of the debate should behave, through policy and statements, in a way that encourages cultural respect and minimizes xenophobia. In addition, they should enact legislation that punishes hateful statements and actions.

4. Governments should encourage education and media programs about other cultures and their specific sensitivities

to build bridges and promote mutual understanding of different cultures and religions.

5. Governments should work harder to overcome failures to promote integration and assimilation in order to forge a civic identity and ameliorate feelings of exclusion and victimization and thus undercut radicalization and intolerance.

References

[1] S. Suri, "Denmark: Politics Infused with Xenophobia, Muslim MP Says," *Global Information Network*, May 4, 2006.

[2] A low-context culture is one in which messages are delivered directly without consideration of accepted cultural customs and mores. A high-context culture is one within which messages are given indirectly without degrading or hurting the feelings of others. "Expert links cartoon incident with cultural differences between states," *Turkish Daily News*, February 7, 2006.

[3] D. Bilefsk, "Cartoon Dispute Promotes Identity Crisis for Liberal Denmark," *The New York Times*, February 12, 2006, p. 1, p. 22.

[4] S. Schwartz, "More Fallout From the Carton Jihad," *The Weekly Standard*, May 29, 2006, Vol. 11, Issue 35, p. 14.

[5] Z. Hussein, "Danish Envoy to Singapore Meets Muslim Groups," *The Straits Times*, February 21, 2006.

CHAPTER 7

OIL, PORTS, AND STEEL: SYMPTOMS OF GLOBAL INSECURITY

GRAEME HERD
NAYEF R.F. AL-RODHAN

Dr. Graeme Herd is Joint Course Director of the International Training Course in Security Policy at the Geneva Centre for Security Policy, Geneva, Switzerland

Dr. Nayef R.F. Al-Rodhan is Senior Scholar in Geostrategy and Director of the Program on the Geopolitical Implications of Globalization and Transnational Security at the Geneva Centre for Security Policy, Geneva, Switzerland

Abstract
The United States (US) rebuffs China over an attempt by the Chinese National Offshore Oil Corporation to take over Unocal. Dubai Ports World fails in its bid to acquire port operations in the US. And Mittal Steel fails to purchase the European steel giant Arcelor. All three of these recent cases can readily be understood within the context of globalization and can be seen as symptoms of an insecure world. The increasing economic penetration of Euro-Atlantic markets and industries (steel, ports, and oil) places stress on a Euro-Atlantic and particularly a US self-perception of economic success and status. It highlights a deep-seated and barely acknowledged Euro-Atlantic resistance to the increasing pace with which economic power is being redistributed toward India and China and its implications: the realities of relative decline. These issues challenge key assumptions that underpin today's globalization (not least the supposed relationship between global economic interdependence and stability) and so begin to identify the contours of the next phase of globalization.

1. Policy Challenges

Dubai Ports World (DP World), Mittal Steel, and the Chinese National Offshore Oil Corporation (CNOOC) all provide high-profile contemporary examples in which Western states have prevented companies in the Middle East, India, and China from buying domestic ones; by doing so, these same Western states have prevented the global economy from operating according to free-market principles, whereby acquisitions should be governed by economic considerations, not political ones. Collectively, these episodes suggest that "economic patriotism" is as much a political response to the perception of untrammeled globalization as it is an economic one. As the dynamics of globalization have undercut the importance and influence of national leaders, these leaders have stressed their patriotic credentials by appearing to "take a stand" in the national interest. Such political posturing has two short-term political virtues: Politicians appear stronger and more effective, and, at the same time, they undercut the source of their diminished status and power (globalization). Ultimately, though, such short-term actions undermine the legitimacy of free-market principles and a liberal economic order – the hallmark of contemporary globalization – and the system that provides more benefits than costs to developed states (if not all developing states as well). This paper demonstrates the tensions, challenges, and dilemmas generated as politics remains national, but economics and security global.

DP World made a $6.8 billion offer to acquire London-based Peninsular & Oriental Steam Navigation Co. (P&O), which controlled five US port terminal facilities.[1] By acquiring P&O, DP World would have assumed control over those port operations. Given the close ties between the US and the United Arab Emirates (UAE) and the fact that US intelligence agencies did not object to the deal, it was expected that the acquisition would proceed. However, in response to fierce opposition from the US Congress, which cited security concerns ("giving Arabs control of our ports" and so imperiling national security), DP World was forced to divest its container terminals in the US. It did so to an American entity in March 2006 after the House Appropriations Committee voted 62-2 to block the deal. The DP World deal came in an election year (the US mid-terms), and this, more than objective security considerations, appears to have politicized the issue.[2]

In mid-2005, US Congressional detractors and Chevron lobbyists forced the CNOOC, China's largest offshore oil producer, out of the running for Unocal, which was eventually taken over by Chevron. Although more than half of Unocal's oil and gas production comes from seven countries outside North America, it was argued that oil and natural gas are strategic assets critical to US national security;

hence, Unocal ought not to be in foreign hands, the argument went. This acquisition would have been the largest international acquisition by a Chinese company.

In line with global consolidation in the steel industry, bankers working for Mittal Steel (headquartered in Amsterdam but run from London), whose chairman is Indian-born Lakshmi Mittal, have made a bid for Arcelor, a Luxembourg-based company, in a move that would create the world's biggest steelmaker, three times larger than its nearest rival.[3] European politicians, particularly parliamentarians in Luxembourg, France, and Spain, have attempted to prevent this acquisition through new anti-takeover measures and have justified these restrictive protectionist practices in terms of "economic patriotism," an expression coined by Dominique de Villepin, France's prime minister.[4]

In May 2006, Arcelor announced plans to merge with a Russian steel company, Severstal, which is run by Aleksei Mordashov. If the merger succeeds, it would create the largest steelmaker in the world and therefore replace Mittal as the industry leader. Joseph Kinsch, Arcelor's chairman, stated that the Russian merger made better sense: "We are close to one another, because we are steel makers and because of our origins.... just like us, [Mordashov] grew up in this business... he's a true European."[5] Such statements have reinforced the perception that the original Arcelor reaction to the Mittal bid was xenophobic and racist. The merger with Severstal would undercut the Mittal bid and create an industry rival instead of an ally. Some analysts have questioned the validity of the deal, and the economic and political implications will most likely have larger policy consequences.

Although Mittal Steel did eventually merge with Arcelor on June 29, 2006, the policy challenges raised by these three closely watched and controversial acquisition attempts center on how to manage growing economic interdependence (which is presumed to increase stability) while avoiding or minimizing politicized reactions that aim to maximize electoral support – in other words, on how to balance objective national economic security benefits with the more subjective political advantage.

2. Responses

Chris Koch, president and chief executive of the World Shipping Council, characterized Congressional efforts to limit foreign ownership of US port terminals as "myopic." Rather, Koch said, the US must include companies such as DP World as partners in efforts to protect the global supply chain: "Congress just told the third-largest terminal operator in the world that it did not trust them. The facts presented did not justify such a judgment of the company."[6] US Homeland Security Secretary Michael Chertoff tried to assure Congressional opponents of the deal that the proposed acquisition of London-based P&O's local ports by DP World would not threaten national security because, as a precondition for the proposed buyout, DP World was committed to cooperating with future port-security initiatives.[7]

As a result of the CNOOC's failed bid, Unocal shareholders lost about $2 billion in comparison with Chevron's lower bid (the CNOOC offered $18.5 billion, a premium compared with the $17.3 billion bid offered by Chevron), and the US executive branch's well-established regulatory framework to deal with foreign acquisitions of US companies was damaged. The CNOOC was set to benefit from a subsidized state loan to fund the acquisition ($7 billion, at low interest), thereby exacerbating concerns that the playing field was not level and encouraging political opposition in the US.[8] The policy response was characterized by the classic "political blame game," as different actors tried to "out-tough" each other by justifying their opposition with references to national strategic interests. Protectionist instincts and politics won the day. After the deal was prevented, policy responses centered on two Congressional proposals aimed at giving the US Committee on Foreign Investment more power over mergers. A bill from Rep. Duncan Hunter, R-Calif., sought to stop foreign companies from owning infrastructure or "systems" vital to national security.[9]

The Mittal Steel issue highlights a rather paradoxical French (and more widely European and even global) attitude towards manipulating the free-market system in favor of national economic interests rather than in accordance with free-market principles. While France is keen for its own multinationals to invest globally and acquire assets abroad, and for foreign firms to create businesses in France, it contests foreign efforts to merge with and then own French firms. Ten major companies on the CAC 40 index of the Paris Bourse are exempt from foreign takeover bids. At the same time, as the Doha Round of international trade negotiations illustrated, China, India, and Brazil are also resisting calls made by developing countries for greater liberalization, as they seek to protect their state-controlled economies and national industries. As Patrick Sabatier, the deputy editor of the Paris daily "Liberation," noted: "Economic patriotism is the flip side of free-market liberalism and part of the current fashion for globalization à la carte."[10]

3. Dilemmas

1. How much security does the Western world want, and how much can it afford? How can greater security be ensured without undermining the global economy and free-market principles? Congressional demands for more powers to review foreign contracts following the DP World bid, for example, risk stifling foreign investment into the US, and policy makers attempting to maximize national security can undermine economic security based on an open investment culture.

2. Moves to increase domestic security can have a negative impact on foreign economic policy and weaken the ability of states to secure their foreign policy objectives. Given that the UAE is a staunch US partner in the region and supports the US in the so-called global war on terror, how can domestic economic security considerations be balanced with broader international security objectives?

3. How can responsible political actors undercut the power of self-indulgent populists who enflame public fears through political theater without isolating themselves from their publics? To what extent must mature actors pander to the worst fears of their electorates and target audiences, and to what extent can they challenge and change public opinion?

4. Implications

Paranoia over the proposed Dubai ports deal and Chinese-owned oil companies and Indian-owned steel companies are proxies for a growing European and American discomfort with globalization. Such angst represents a generalized fear of foreigners squeezing out US and European corporations and taking employment from middle-class workers who have experienced the phenomenon of growth without job or wage increases. This reaction is not completely new to the US. In the 1980s, at a time when the US economy was also struggling, Japan was viewed in much the same light when attempting to purchase large buildings in New York.

This reaction also reflects a deep insecurity about globalization and its implications: a process over which Euro-Atlantic governments feel they have lost control and are now increasingly vulnerable to the forces they have unleashed.[11] As a result, political elites in the US and Europe are increasingly willing to securitize issues – "soft on terrorism," "soft on US jobs" – in order to gain political advantage, and this increases pressures toward isolationism and nationalism. The backlash against globalization is justified by claims of state exceptionalism and the promotion of "national champions." Such a policy approach, paradoxically, increases the danger of nationalism being reignited even as globalization downgrades the importance of states. It feeds the growing xenophobia that is currently felt in the US due to the security crisis in Iraq and the current standing of the US economy.

Since the US has no experience with state-owned companies, the bid by DP World naturally caused many negative reactions about the possibility of a foreign, state-run company taking control of a number of US ports. While it is true that, if this company were not state-owned, the government probably still would have opposed it, the reaction would have most likely been much less severe.

There is a common perception that state-owned and state-run Chinese energy firms are one and the same and that both are vehicles of Beijing's foreign policy in the field of energy. However, the owners of the CNOOC would argue they are state-owned but independently run and not a foreign policy instrument. Regardless of the relationship, it is difficult to accurately forecast the implications of the Unocal episode on how China will exert its influence on the global oil market in the long run.

The Mittal Steel issue has drawn accusations of racism and discrimination from India. Indian Commerce and Industry Minister Kamal Nath stated: "We have told [the French authorities] that [skin] colour and nationality should not be… criteria in such deals... [they]

should be [made] on the basis of purely commercial considerations."[12] Although French Trade Minister Christine Lagarde was quick to assure India that Paris did not discriminate on the basis of skin color, nationality, or race, the perception of double standards in attitudes to globalization was apparent. This attitude appears universal: France did not object to the acquisition of a French firm by another European company; India would not be open to a major investment by a company owned by Pakistan's government. Such restrictions on cross-border investments in the global marketplace only hinder development and economic growth.

5. Future Trajectories/Scenarios

The issues touched on in this policy brief are likely to become even more accentuated in future phases of globalization that even now appear to be characterized by a scarcity of energy supplies, increasing competition for these resources, and accelerating climate change.[13] The way in which the high-profile takeover bids examined in this policy brief were politicized by state elites and non-state actors in 2005 and 2006 challenges the notion that increasing economic interdependence among the world's economies through globalization enhances their stability.

US strategic interests weakened: Long-term consequences for the US include damage to its strategic interests and the possibility of destabilizing global markets. The way in which the US reacted demonstrated that it was afraid of terrorism, that it did not trust Muslims, and that it was prepared to alienate and then abandon an ally (UAE) when put under pressure. This reaction also has the potential to weaken the US dollar as a major currency, as it stigmatized and undercut the basis upon which the dollar maintains its value: the fact that it offers a wide range of investment choices and opportunities. If foreigners decide that their cash is better spent elsewhere, then this could damage prospects for US growth.[14] The present economic order is largely an artifact of US actions following World War II, one that was constructed to serve US interests but that no longer works only to the advantage of the US. If the US uses inward-looking protectionist measures to insulate its economy, this will damage globalization, which is based on a liberal international order and free-market economies (underpinned, for example, by the World Trade Organization (WTO)), and may cause its retreat.

EU protectionism increasing: Europe's leading business lobby group has claimed that industrialists want stronger political leadership in the event of sensitive takeover battles, such as Mittal Steel's hostile bid for Arcelor. Ernest-Antoine Seilliere, head of Union des Industries de la Communauté européenne (UNICE), a European employers federation, said that there had been "no meaningful political answer" to the Mittal bid at the European level, only national responses from Belgium, France, Luxembourg, and Spain. He suggested that a stronger sense of political direction was needed and that, without a stronger EU voice, "business [would] become less interested in what's happening in this part of the world." Steel, he argued, was a symbolic industry whose future had sparked great passion – the Mittal bid was "a symbol of globalization against a symbol of Europeanization."[15] It would be paradoxical if such a reaction were to become more widespread: states consolidate into regional economic blocs in order to protect themselves against the perceived encroachment that globalization poses for national economic independence.

6. Policy Recommendations

In general, policies need to be developed that center on the implementation of awareness-raising campaigns to increase recognition among policy makers, politicians, the media, civil society, and ordinary people of the dilemmas associated with each aspect of globalization. Globalization carries with it the triggers that can cause a backlash against the processes it promotes.

1. In the US, political-marketing and public-relations mistakes need to be rectified. The US administration should have demonstrated the nature and integrity of its review process in order to undercut allegations and political posturing by politicians. Transparency of the review process was needed. In the case of DP World, the administration should have stated more forcefully that how ports examine incoming goods – the competence and prerogative of the US Customs and Coast Guard and Department of Homeland Security – is much more important than which commercial administration owns the port facilities. Unless this action is taken, policy becomes a random expression of political expediency,

hypocrisy, and unthinking emotionalism, which damages trade relations, relations with allies, and the pursuit of strategic objectives.

2. Governments should promote actions and arguments that can inform US and European media, politicians, and the general public on the incoherence of arguments that support the idea of patriotic criteria for takeovers. Protectionism harms Euro-Atlantic economies, and it hinders the sale of their goods to emerging markets in countries like China, India, Brazil, thus decreasing global stability.
   a) "Could French giants be good for Europe, but European giants bad for France? That is a hard motto to sell."[16]

   b) Alan Johnson, UK trade and industry secretary, rather pointedly warned against trying "to repel the surge of globalization by creating a Fortress UK or a Fortress Europe. There are advocates of protectionism amongst some of our closest European neighbors. Measures to protect key industries from foreign takeovers where there are no state security issues are futile and self-defeating. The paradox of protectionism is that it destroys what it seeks to protect."

   c) Gerard Augustin-Normand, president of Richelieu Finances and an Arcelor shareholder, said political interference in the proposed bid by Mittal Steel did "no credit to our country" and noted: "Fund managers need to consider the offer in all independence – beyond philosophical, religious and political concerns. The only context is the price."[17]

   d) One analyst noted with regard to US responses to the DP World deal: "the world's largest economy was prepared to change the rules, undermining its investment credibility and signaling to others that this type of parochial behavior is acceptable."[18]

e) Stephen Roach, chief economist of investment bank Morgan Stanley, raised concern over the negative impact of rising American protectionism on Sino-US relations and the global economy. "The Sino-US relations are perhaps the world's most important bilateral economic relationship in the 21st century. That relationship is now at risk, and if not attended to it could backfire, with significant negative impact on China, the United States, and the broader global economy."[19]

f) Kamal Nath, India's trade and industry minister, said: "This is an era of globalization, cross-border investment and liberalization, not one in which investors are judged by the color of their skin in breach of... national treatment rules. If the color of the shareholder, the nationality of the shareholder, or the passport of the shareholder is to be looked at, then we will have to give new definitions to national treatment." He argued that governments should allow shareholders to determine a bid's outcome and that, "Countries must wake up to the new economic architecture."[20]

3. Foreign companies can also learn lessons and change their approaches to the US. Assistant Secretary of State for Near Eastern Affairs David Welch noted: "Did we learn some lessons from this? I think absolutely. The American administration has to be careful to make a more convincing case about issues such as foreign investment in strategic areas. And our foreign partners likewise want to pay attention to the political environment in the United States and to make presentations in a way that is responsive to that political environment."[21] Chinese companies, for example, need to heed and manage public opinion for sensitive transactions in order to try to not remain hostage to the larger dynamic of Sino-international relations, over which they have little sway.

References

[1] The ports were: The Port of New York/New Jersey, The Port of Philadelphia, The Maryland Port of Baltimore, The Port of Miami, and The Port of New Orleans.

[2] N. Kumar, "Has globalisation gone too far," *The Financial Express*, March 28, 2006.

[3] P. Marsh, "Mittal comes under pressure to improve bid for Arcelor," *Financial Times*, April 17, 2006, p. 18; S. Liatner and P. Marsh, "Steel hardens opinions in Luxembourg," *Financial Times*, March 22, 2006, p. 26.

[4] J. Plender, "Europe feels the toxic effect of corporate nationalism," *Financial Times*, April 6, 2006, p. 19.

[5] H. Timmons, J. Kanter, and A.E. Kramer, "Arcelor Offers Deal to Russian Steel Giant," *International Herald Tribune*, May 26, 2006, see http://www.iht.com/articles/2006/05/26/business/arcelor.php.

[6] "Koch: Don't limit foreign investment in US ports," *Shipping Digest*, April 10, 2006.

[7] R. Block, "Chertoff Says U.S. Ports Takeover Would Tighten Grip on Security," *The Wall Street Journal*, March 7, 2006.

[8] P. Parry, J. McCreery, A. Del Maestro, and B.A. Hamilton, "Opinion: UNOCAL: A Bump in the Road," *Petroleum Economist*, April 11, 2006, p. 32.

[9] J.N. Hoover, "Politicians Missed The Memo That Global Tech Has Arrived," *InformationWeek*, April 3, 2006, p. 26.

[10] "France's Economic Patriotism," *The Statesman*, May 21, 2006.

[11] P. Stevens, "A perilous collision between nationalism and globalization," *Financial Times*, March 3, 2006, p. 17.

[12] PTI news agency, New Delhi, June 1, 2006.

[13] "Mapping the Global Future: Report of the National Intelligence Council's 2020 Project," Washington, DC: NIC 2004-13, Dec. 2004; J. Gray, "The Global Delusion," *The New York Review of Boo*ks, Vol. 53, No. 7, April 27, 2006.

[14] "When nations get overprotective," *Investment Adviser*, February 27, 2006.

[15] G. Parker, "Mittal bid shows need for 'strong EU role'," *Financial Times*, February 6, 2006, p. 8.

[16] D. Moisi, "'Economic patriotism' will be Europe's undoing," *Financial Times*, March 6, 2006, p. 19.

[17] C. Adams, P. Hollinger, and P. Marsh, "UK attacks French line on protectionism," *Financial Times*, February 2, 2006, p. 29.

[18] "Dubai Ports Debacle Will Return To Haunt An Over-protective US - Protectionism And Nationalism Can Only Harm The Reputation Of Developed Countries That Use Them To Retain The Status Quo," *The Banker*, April 1, 2006.

[19] "US Economists hit out at American Protectionism," *Business Daily Update*, March 21, 2006.

[20] J. Johnson, P. Marsh, and R. Minder, "Racism alleged over Mittal's Arcelor bid," *Financial Times*, February 11, 2006, p. 1.

[21] C. Stratford, "US official: No longlasting fallout over DP World issue," *Gulf News*, March 30, 2006.

CHAPTER 8

POTENTIAL OUTCOMES OF MIGRATION FLUX IN A GLOBALIZED WORLD AND ITS SECURITY IMPLICATIONS

SLOBODAN DJAJIC

Dr. Slobodan Djajic is Professor of International Economics at the Graduate Institute of International Studies, Geneva, Switzerland

Abstract
This policy brief examines the challenges presented by the expanding potential for international migration in an increasingly globalized world economy. The focus is on ways to enable host countries to take advantage of the economic opportunities that migration offers while minimizing the threats to individual, group, and national security that uncontrolled migration may represent.

1. Policy Challenges

One of the key challenges facing the world economy in the 21st century is how to enjoy the benefits of international migration while effectively managing the associated risks. The existing international wage and labor-productivity gaps reflect the large potential gains that are not being realized due to barriers to international migration. While these gaps have been expanding over the last couple of decades, the communications revolution and the declining real cost of transport have lowered obstacles to international migration, making it an attractive option for millions of people living in the developing world.

Uncontrolled immigration flows, however, are not desirable from the point of view of both the source and the destination countries. For the source countries, an obvious problem is the loss of skilled workers who would be among the first to leave, depriving their countries of a key ingredient in the process of social, economic, and institutional development. From the perspective of the host countries, uncontrolled migration also represents a threat to economic security for many of its citizens. It can give rise to a substantial decline in the real income of labor and potentially overburden the existing infrastructure and provision of social services. It can also create social and possibly ethnic and racial tensions as real income is redistributed among factor owners due to changes in commodity and factor prices that stem from a large increase in the supply of labor.

In an effort to control growing immigration pressures, advanced countries have been tightening controls on immigration. The rising barriers to legal immigration over the last three decades have produced increased illegal immigration. The advanced countries do, however, need and want some immigrants. The demographics of declining fertility rates and population aging are contributing to growing shortages in the labor market. These can be partly addressed through the process of automation, increased imports of labor-intensive goods, outsourcing of production, greater participation of women in the labor force, and other ways of reducing the demand for and increasing the supply of labor. Immigrant workers are, nonetheless, needed to fill the remaining gap. They are also needed to help support welfare states, which offer generous benefits to residents of the advanced countries. With the ratio of tax-paying workers to non-working residents steadily declining, immigration (particularly of the guest-worker type) can play a role in reducing budgetary strains and postponing tax increases that can have a negative effect on the growth prospects of the advanced countries.

2. Responses

The advanced countries have pursued policies to restrict what they consider to be unwanted immigration, essentially the inflows of unskilled labor from Asia, Africa, and Central and South America, while encouraging immigration of certain categories of skilled labor, particularly information technology (IT) specialists and health workers. Recent efforts to restrict immigration of unskilled labor have included not only tighter border controls and internal enforcement measures and stricter asylum and visa policies, but also international cooperation in monitoring and controlling illegal immigration flows. The need for unskilled immigrant labor, however, has given rise to political pressures that have limited enforcement budgets as well as the capacity of enforcement agencies to restrict employer access to undocumented workers and to apprehend and deport illegal aliens.[1] In consequence, the stock of undocumented foreign workers has been growing in the advanced countries, and so has the degree of dependency of certain sectors on such workers. A number of advanced countries have responded to these market and political pressures by establishing guest-worker programs with specific partner countries.

Amnesties have also been tried, enabling illegal aliens in some cases to become permanent residents and eventually citizens (1986 Immigration Reform and Control Act (IRCA) amnesty in the USA) or legalized guest workers (as in some of the Western European countries). While amnesties produce a one-time reduction in the stock of illegal aliens, they also tend to encourage illegal immigration by creating expectations of future amnesties. In that sense, they can actually be counterproductive in dealing with the problem in the long run.

3. Dilemmas

Since 9/11 and the coordinated bombings in Madrid and London, there is a growing concern in the host countries over the potential threat to security from its own immigrant population. This relates not only to newly arrived legal and illegal immigrants, but also to second- and third-generation youths who are having difficulties in assimilating into the socio-economic mainstream of the host-country society. This type of security threat is not new, but it grows in significance when the host country is involved in a major, protracted international conflict.

Another type of security threat arises from international migration in the form of refugee flows. This is particularly the case in underdeveloped regions, where the host countries are unable to meet such flows with adequate resources. Refugees then compete directly with the local population for scarce resources, cause environmental degradation, and generate other negative externalities that are a threat to economic security. More concrete security threats arise where refugee flows are accompanied by international flows of arms, fighters, and ideologies that contribute to spreading of conflict throughout the region, both within and between states.[2] A refugee inflow can also affect the ethnic balance within a country. If the ethnic balance is already delicate, this can easily generate instability and spark conflicts.

Rapid growth in the stock of economic migrants in the countries with ethnically homogeneous populations can also produce tensions between immigrants and the natives. This is particularly true if the inflows seem to be imposed by external factors and the benefits of immigration are perceived to be small. Discrimination against immigrants is often observed in such cases. When it occurs in the labor market, it has a negative impact on the rate of return on human capital of immigrants, discouraging them and their children from investing in human capital formation. This reduces the pace of economic assimilation and contributes to further polarization, tensions, and conflict. Discrimination against immigrants in other dimensions is similarly damaging to the assimilation process.

Illegal immigration presents security concerns, as well. It reflects the host country's inability to secure its border and exercise its sovereignty over who is permitted to enter and work in the country. Not being able to identify or locate individuals residing in the economy is another dimension of the same problem. Moreover, when internal enforcement of laws prohibiting employment of illegal aliens is lax, it effectively discriminates against law-abiding employers. This encourages them to respond to competitive pressures by also violating the law and hiring clandestine foreign workers. On the other hand, when access of employers to undocumented labor is highly restricted, illegal aliens are further marginalized and encouraged to explore criminal opportunities. Thus, illegal immigration does present a threat to security and law and order in a number of different dimensions. Finally, there is the problem of economic security, alluded to earlier. So the key issue from the security perspective of the advanced countries is how to take advantage of international migration in addressing the anticipated future shortages in the labor market, while minimizing the security risks associated with migration flows.

4. Implications

Addressing these problems of host countries requires policies at the national and international levels that allow for controlled and registered inflows of needed immigrants while effectively blocking transactions in the labor market for those who violate the laws. It also calls for effective policies to end discrimination and racism, which also allow immigrants to feel welcome and fully protected in the host country, in the labor market and elsewhere. It requires that the international community shows more generosity and determination in dealing with and preventing refugee crises, as well as in addressing some of the key economic problems of the developing countries that are fueling immigration pressures.

5. Future Trajectories/Scenarios

If current policies continue without major modifications, the demographic and wage differentials between the advanced and the developing countries will continue to swell the ranks of those attempting to migrate. The growing demand for primary commodities (including metals and energy products) associated with the rapid growth of the large emerging economies is likely to increase competition for control of natural resources throughout the world economy. This can contribute to instability in the resource-rich developing countries and increase the likelihood of internal and international conflicts. On top of the other factors that have been contributing to refugee flows over the past couple of decades, it is safe to assume that they will continue to grow.

The established immigrant communities and networks in the advanced countries will serve to facilitate the inflows, job acquisition, and settlement of newcomers, regardless of whether they are legal immigrants, asylum seekers, or undocumented aliens. At the same time tighter border controls have not been effective over the last two decades in keeping illegal immigrants from arriving at their destinations. When international borders are physically more difficult to cross, innovative new methods are developed by migrants (and those who assist them) in order to meet the challenge.[3] It is also interesting to note that recent efforts by the US authorities to make it more costly to cross the US-Mexico border have transformed many of the *temporary* illegal aliens into *permanent* illegal residents.[4] Prior to the tightening of border controls in the late 1980s and the 1990s, Mexican migrants moved back and forth, depending on the seasonal factors that influence the demand for labor in the southwest of the United States. After the tightening, they switched to a strategy of staying longer in the US, moving further inland to avoid deportation, and bringing their family to the US, as well. Internal enforcement measures have also been ineffective, particularly in the US, but also in Western Europe. In practice, it is very difficult to penalize politically powerful employers and industries for hiring illegal aliens when they have difficulty in finding documented workers to fill the jobs.

6. Policy Recommendations

Addressing the problem of unwanted immigration, securing national borders, gaining control over who is allowed to reside and work in the country, preventing conflicts between immigrants and natives, while at the same time meeting the growing demand for foreign labor requires a significant overhaul of immigration policies and enforcement strategies in the advanced countries. Any new policy initiative would have to account for the market forces that have been fueling illegal immigration over the last couple of decades. To take the US as an example, establishment of a guest-worker program is an essential component of a policy package that deals with labor market shortages, reduces the stock of illegal immigrants, and lowers migration pressures in the long run. A key element in any such program must be the incentive for migrant workers to return to, but also consume and invest in their countries of origin. To reduce migration pressures, the non-migrants of the sending countries must benefit from the activities of their compatriots employed abroad. There are a number of ways in which they can benefit. The spending of remittances on locally produced goods and services, the transfer of technology and skills through return migration, and investments by migrants in local business activity, all serve to improve the prospects for economic growth in the sending countries. Without that growth and development, the expanding migration pressures and illegal immigration flows cannot be addressed in the long run.

To deal with some of the security concerns, applicants for guest-worker status can be vetted against national security criteria and then issued counterfeit-proof guest-worker ID cards in their home countries, where they should also be able to renew them, provided they hold a steady job in the host country. To encourage guest workers to return and contribute to development at home (through their expenditures, skills, and investment of accumulated savings), there should be at least some restrictions on bringing family members to the host country. There should also be a fee charged for the issuance of a guest-worker ID (in lieu of fees currently charged by alien smugglers), which should be refundable with interest in the source country on the condition that the guest worker respects the guidelines of the program.

Pension benefits should also be payable to guest-workers in the source country. To encourage employers to first seek unemployed permanent residents and citizens, levies should be imposed on hiring guest workers, with revenues redistributed to returning migrants in the form of return benefits payable in the source country. With the establishment of a well-functioning guest-worker program, it becomes both technically and politically feasible to enforce restrictions on illegal immigration and deny labor market access to both illegal immigrants and their employers. It is also important to note that effective border control can be achieved more efficiently with the cooperation of the country's neighbors. Neighboring countries should be given privileged status in a guest-worker program to facilitate cooperation in regulating guest-worker flows and controlling unauthorized immigration, including that from third countries.

In trying to reduce illegal immigration, the advanced countries must also recognize that they are not competitive in many of the labor-intensive manufacturing and agricultural activities. Protection of those sectors by means of restrictive trade policies and subsidy schemes deprives developing countries of markets, growth opportunities, and jobs for workers who would prefer to remain in their country rather than do the same jobs abroad as illegal aliens.

Admission of *permanent* immigrants seems to work best when governed by some variant of a points system, designed to select immigrants on the basis of characteristics associated with economic success in the host country.[5] If immigration policies ensure that those admitted are an asset for the host country, there will be more public satisfaction with the immigration system, less xenophobia, and less discrimination against immigrants, although active policies to prevent discrimination and educate natives about the benefits of immigration are urgently needed in most of the host countries.

In sum, new measures are needed to achieve the following broad objectives:

1. Facilitate the required immigration flows in an orderly and secure manner;
2. Reduce the scope for illegal immigration by providing well-structured legal alternatives;
3. Assure fair treatment of immigrants;
4. Create confidence of citizens in national immigration policies; and

5. Address the long-term goal of eliminating illegal immigration by supporting trade and migration policies that contribute to expansion of employment opportunities in the developing countries.

References

[1] P. Martin and M. Miller, "Employer Sanctions: French, German and U.S. Experiences," International Labor Office, Geneva, 2000, available at http://www.ilo.org/public/english/protection/migrant/download/research/imp/imp36.pdf#search='Sanctions%3A%20French%2C%20German%20and%20US%20Experiences%E2%80%9D'.

[2] Salehyan and Gleditsch (2006) find that the presence of refugees from a neighboring country increases the probability of conflict within the host country. See I. Salehyan and K.S. Gleditsch, "Refugees and the Spread of Civil War," *International Organization,* Vol. 60, No. 2, Spring 2006. Also see A. Dowty and G. Loescher, "Refugee Flows as Grounds for International Action," *International Security*, Vol. 21, 1996 and M. Weiner "Security, Stability and International Migration," *International Security*, Vol. 17, 1992-93 for analysis of links between refugee inflows and host-country security.

[3] S. Djajic, "Illegal Immigration: Trends, Policies and Economic Effects," in S. Djajic, (ed.), *International Migration: Trends, Policies and Economic Impact* (London: Routledge, 2001).

[4] S. Djajic, "Dynamics of Immigration Control," *Journal of Population Economics*, Vol. 12, 1999.

[5] G. Borjas, *Heaven's Door* (Princeton: Princeton University Press: 1999).

CHAPTER 9

EDITORIAL OF POLICY BRIEF ON POTENTIAL OUTCOMES OF MIGRATION FLUX IN A GLOBALIZED WORLD AND ITS SECURITY IMPLICATIONS

NAYEF R.F. AL-RODHAN

Dr. Nayef R.F. Al-Rodhan is Senior Scholar in Geostrategy and Director of the Program on the Geopolitical Implications of Globalization and Transnational Security at the Geneva Centre for Security Policy, Geneva, Switzerland

1. Review and Critique

While migration has occurred throughout human history, we are currently in a period in which significant and growing numbers of people are on the move. As a result, international migration can often cause unease and tension. In recent years, immigration has become elevated to a national security issue in many countries in the West. Part of the reason for this is linked to the ambiguity surrounding the social, economic, and cultural consequences of immigration. In Europe, the end of the Cold War focused attention on "new" threats to security, including international migration. The response has often been alarmist, in part because law enforcement agencies have been important in framing the agenda. The 9/11 attacks, as well as those in Madrid and London, have also heightened the salience of international migration in security discourse.[1] Examples of "securitized immigration" include, for instance, a sharp increase in border controls and the concept of a link between immigration and terrorism.

For policy makers, the difficulty is to balance the need for immigration with the security challenges it can present. Many countries are dependent upon imported skilled and unskilled labor. This is especially the case given changing demographic trends in many developed countries, which are facing a shortage of labor and difficulties in funding public pensions, for example. International migration can, therefore, play a role in easing the budgetary strains on developed countries, as well as filling gaps in the labor force.

However, uncontrolled immigration presents a problem for receiving countries. Slobodan Djajic identifies several challenges posed by the expanding potential for international migration for host countries in a globalizing world.[2] He notes that unsolicited migration can result in nationalistic and racist responses from within the host country populations as indigenous populaces perceive, rightly or wrongly, that their jobs are at risk.[3] Unsolicited migration may also result in a reduction in wages for some segments of the host country's population and the social welfare system may come under strain, as well. In the source countries, imigration can also result in a loss of skilled workers, which not only means that the country loses some of its "best and brightest" professionals, who were trained at the expense of their countries of origin, but also that the donor countries' prospects for development are reduced.

Illegal immigration can also adversely affect human security. Many people are willing to put themselves at great risk in attempting to enter host countries illegally and are extremely vulnerable to human trafficking. Moreover, those who survive these often perilous journeys are more likely to be exposed to dangerous working conditions and abuse than workers with permits.

In addition, Djajic highlights that an increasing number of host countries have responded to the challenges they face by tightening immigration controls. States around the world, especially in the West, are cracking down on immigration, even increasing restrictions on legal immigrants and visitors. Ironically, these efforts have often led to undesired outcomes, namely illegal immigration.

In short, Djajic addresses an important aspect of the globalization debate, namely the linkage between immigration and security. Increased accessibility to affordable transport and increased possibilities for communication have rendered migration attractive and feasible for many individuals. At the same time, however, unsolicited immigration raises a number of concerns, both for host and source countries.

2. Dilemmas and Our Recommendations

International immigration presents both opportunities as well as challenges for states. What the correct policy framework should be remains highly contested, as governments often face alarmist media campaigns that make it difficult to address the issue in a balanced

way. How governments respond to immigration needs and related policy areas will be crucial in achieving prosperity, maintaining generous social welfare systems, and nurturing good inter-cultural relations. We highlight eight dilemmas related to this issue area and eight corresponding recommendations that may contribute to appropriate policy choices.

The policy dilemmas and recommendations presented here are directly linked to policy challenges currently faced by governments across the globe. One of the most formidable challenges that governments face is reconciling the need for foreign labor in order to successfully manage the consequences of lower birth rates and aging populations in the West with the anxieties and tensions that an increased presence of people from unfamiliar cultures necessarily implies. Without adequate policy responses from governments, immigration – whether legal or illegal – may result in increased tensions between immigrant communities and dominant national groups within host countries. This may, in turn, lead to feelings of alienation among immigrant communities or threats to their human or societal security,[4] and even conflict. It is thus vital for countries not only to develop open, targeted immigration policies, but also to develop and implement policies aimed at recognizing the long-term social, cultural, and economic contributions of migration.

An additional issue for policy makers is the need to promote legal immigration and to prevent illegal immigration, human trafficking, abuse, and criminality without infringing on civil liberties and human rights. Following 9/11, for example, the atmosphere of fear in some countries meant that many migrants were afraid to speak out about alleged violations of their civil liberties by over-enthusiastic law enforcement agencies.[5] This will require an open, targeted immigration policy that minimizes the impulse for illegal migration, while making a distinction between legal and illegal immigrants.

Another dilemma mentioned earlier is the need to balance the needs of developed countries against those of developing countries. The prosperity of both depends upon well-conceived immigration policies in the developed world. Policies should be conceived in such a way as to ensure that migration results in a net gain for all involved. Djajic, for example, suggests that immigration policies should give migrant workers an incentive to return to, as well as to consume and invest in, their countries of origin. He also proposes that this might be achieved by encouraging migrants to spend remittances on locally produced goods and services, the transfer of technology and skills through return migration, and investments by migrants in local business activities, to improve the development prospects in their home countries.

3. Conclusion

History has long included migratory movements that have benefited the advancement of humankind. The increased incentive for migration contributes to the capacity of states around the world to attain sustained economic growth and prosperity and, as such economic security. However, if not managed effectively, migration can negatively affect not only economic security but also human and societal security. The challenge is to encourage states to develop targeted immigration policies that minimize the incentives for illegal immigration, as well as tensions between host and immigrant populations, and to cooperate effectively with other states to reduce illicit immigration and human trafficking.

References

[1] J.C. Ross, "Securitizing Migration after 11 March," *Real Instituto Elcano de Estudios Internacionales y Estratégicos*, March 2004, http://www.realinstitutoelcano.org/analisis/460/ARI-56-2004-I.pdf#search='Securitizing%20Migration%20after%2011%20March'.

[2] For the brief in its entirety, please see Chapter 8.

[3] P. Hough, *Understanding Global Security* (London and New York: Routledge, 2004), p. 109.

[4] *Ibid.*

[5] Ross, o*p. cit.,* note 1, p. 4.

CHAPTER 10

US HEGEMONY AND GLOBALIZATION

MARK S. SHEETZ

Dr. Mark Sheetz is Faculty Member at the Geneva Centre for Security Policy, Geneva, Swtizerland

Abstract
The power and influence of the United States (US) is now the defining feature of world affairs. Indeed, the United States is a hegemonic power insofar as it has been able to impose its set of rules on the international system. The US also provides public goods to the system, such as an international economic, commercial, and financial order and a global political and security order. If globalization amounts to the opening up of national borders to foreign economic, political, and cultural influence, then globalization serves an American vision of world order. What will happen to globalization without the foundation of American hegemonic power? Pressures to reverse political and economic reform may grow, and the forces of protectionism in both its economic and political forms may revive. This paper argues that globalization is the product of a particular set of structural conditions. It is an epiphenomenon of American hegemony, which created and nurtures it. As such, globalization cannot be sustained without US hegemony and will persist only as long as the United States remains the world's only superpower.

1. Policy Challenges

The power and pervasive influence of the United States (US) is now the defining feature of world affairs. One American aircraft carrier battle group can project more force than most of the world's armies put together. The nuclear-powered aircraft carrier "USS Enterprise" is as high as a 25-story building. It has a crew of 5,600, with 85 combat aircraft, and can travel halfway around the world in two weeks. As a rule, its taskforce includes two Aegis-class cruisers to protect it from incoming aircraft and missiles, four frigates and destroyers to protect it from surface ships, two Los Angeles-class nuclear attack submarines to protect it from enemy submarines, and several amphibious assault ships carrying battalions of Marine expeditionary forces, their accompanying helicopters, and landing craft. A carrier battle group is virtually indestructible. Its full complement comprises some 15,000 personnel. Its aircraft alone can strike up to 700 targets in a single day within an accuracy of 1 meter. There is no equivalent in the world to its concentration of offensive military power. The United States does not just have one of these battle groups, it has 12 of them.[1]

The United States economy produces over 30 percent of total world product. Some 70 percent of all Nobel laureates in the sciences, economics, and medicine conduct their research in America. The United States alone accounts for roughly 50 percent of all Internet traffic. The world's leading firms in the fields of information technology, biotechnology, and nanotechnology are American. American universities are the envy of the Earth, and American language, films, and culture permeate the globe.[2] The US deploys forces in more than 125 countries worldwide. It spends a mere 3 percent of gross domestic product (GDP) on defense, and yet its defense budget surpasses the military expenditures of all other countries in the world combined.[3] As the historian Paul Kennedy has noted: "Nothing has ever existed like this disparity of power … Charlemagne's empire was merely Western European in its reach. The Roman empire stretched farther afield, but there was another great empire in Persia, and a larger one in China."[4]

Insofar as it is able to impose its set of rules on the international system, the United States is a hegemonic power.[5] But hegemons do not merely set the rules of the system, they also supply public goods to provide an incentive for other nations to accept those rules. A public good, like clean air and water, is one in whose costs one cannot be forced to share and from whose benefits one cannot be excluded. Because of the logic of collective action, international public goods – like a monetary system, free trade, or global security – will not be provided unless there is one party willing to absorb disproportionate costs.[6] For the current international system, that party is the United States. The US pays a disproportionate cost to supply public goods because it derives a disproportionate benefit from enticing other members of the international community to play by its rules. Those goods include a global economic and financial order based on free trade (World Trade Organization), the free flow of capital (International Bank for Reconstruction and Development), and flexible exchange rates (International Monetary Fund), a global political order based on self-determination and human rights (United Nations), and a global security order enforced by American power (North Atlantic Treaty Organisation (NATO)).

If globalization refers to the impact of foreign influences across national borders, be they economic, political, societal, cultural, or information-related, then globalization, in one sense, amounts to little more than an expression of US hegemony. Since the latter part of the 19th century, the United States has advocated an open-door policy that seeks to maintain access to foreign markets and prevent colonial powers from making third countries their own private preserve.[7] More recently, American presidents from both parties have promoted the value of free markets and free societies. Competition is the very soul of the American ethos. In a world of capitalist competition for economic markets and of democratic competition for political ideas, Americans have home-court advantage. Since Woodrow Wilson, US policy has sought to remake the world in America's image. With its modern version of the open door and its penetration of sovereign state markets and cultures, globalization essentially serves to fulfill an American vision of world order.[8]

2. Responses

American forces protect Europe and Asia from a potentially destructive cycle of security competition and arms races. Without the stability afforded by American hegemony, Germany and other European states might feel the need to develop their own nuclear deterrents. The same is true for Japan and its Asian neighbors.[9] The American military presence in the Middle East serves to ensure the free flow of oil to industrial nations at reasonable prices. This commitment began in the wake of the 1973 oil shock and continued in the wake of the Iranian revolution, after President Carter announced that "an attempt by any outside force to gain control of the Persian Gulf region will be regarded as an assault on the vital interests of the United States of America, and such an assault will be repelled by any means necessary, including military force."[10] The US maintains its commitment to the free flow of oil through its protection of Saudi Arabia. This was the motivation for wars against the Iraqi regime of Saddam Hussein in both 1991 and 2003.[11]

US hegemony also serves to control the proliferation of nuclear weapons through a combination of military intervention and diplomatic pressure on "rogue" regimes like Libya, Iraq, Iran, and North Korea. America, it seems, is indeed "the indispensable nation," as Madeleine Albright contended.[12] A recent quote by an Egyptian diplomat is telling: "I cannot succeed in pursuing my domestic objectives, economic or political, and I cannot succeed in pursuing my global objectives -- be it on social issues, on arms control issues, on economic issues -- without engaging America."[13] The larger question is whether there is an alternative to American hegemony.[14] As far as President Bush is concerned, "the only alternative to American leadership is a dramatically more dangerous and anxious world."[15]

3. Dilemmas

The United States would prefer to extend and maintain its hegemony with a minimum of exertion and with a maximum of acceptance from other states. It has thus been willing to facilitate the diffusion of technological innovation, economic prosperity, and organizational skills on a global scale. But the consequence of this diffusion is to allow potential rivals to take advantage of the hegemon's "generosity" and build up indigenous capabilities. This process creates a dynamic of differential growth rates that ultimately results in the emergence of challengers.[16] And challenges to American hegemony in the realm of economic affairs are already visible. Or the American public may grow weary of the costs of maintaining an international gendarmerie and continual military intervention. They may begin to question the cost-benefit calculus and conclude that the benefits of sustaining an open international system are meager.[17] The days of American hegemony would then be numbered. What would happen to globalization in that case? Does globalization depend on US hegemony? Can it continue without the foundation of American hegemonic power? Or is globalization like a genie that has been let out of the bottle, free to take on a life of its own?

4. Implications

Many believe that globalization is synonymous with Americanization. Pressure for liberalization and political reform in Middle Eastern countries is blamed on the United States. The cultural imperialism of the American film industry is decried in Europe. And the threat to French cuisine by the invasion of McDonald's has become a *cause celèbre* in France. Likewise, many believe that the advance of globalization is inexorable, that the growing openness of markets for goods and services and the rising level of international capital mobility cannot be reversed. But the forces of protectionism and economic nationalism, like certain resistant strains of a virus, are surprisingly resilient. Mercantilist impulses are never very far from the surface. And historical precedents exist for such a reversal. During the interwar period, the seemingly irresistible momentum for ever-greater economic interdependence was stopped in its tracks. "Time and again," as Benjamin Cohen observes, "governments have demonstrated their willingness to limit market openness, sacrificing the benefits of globalization, when deemed necessary for the sake of national security, cultural preservation, or environmental protection."[18] Pressure for limitations on trade and capital flows is again growing in the American Congress. If the United States either withdraws voluntarily from its dominant role in the world or is forced to scale back through a combination of military and economic overextension, it is hard to see how globalization will be sustained.

5. Future Trajectories/Scenarios

With its willingness to absorb unimaginably high deficits in its balance of trade, the United States acts as the global market of last resort. With its willingness to provide exceptional financial backing to the International Monetary Fund, the United States acts as the global lender of last resort. And with its willingness to intervene militarily and to provide disaster relief in international crises, the United States acts as the underwriter of a global insurance policy against catastrophes. Without an American hegemon to sustain a liberal economic system, one might expect an increase in barriers to unfettered economic penetration of national borders. Difficulties in the current round of World Trade Organization (WTO) talks are characteristic of the constant struggle waged by free traders against protectionist impulses. Without a global American military presence, one might expect increasing resistance to the unfettered spread of liberal political reforms, like democracy and the rights of women and minorities. One might also anticipate less pressure for standardization. English may not necessarily remain the *lingua franca* of business, air-traffic control, and diplomacy, and globally recognized standards in the areas of communication, transportation, and technology may be harder to come by.

6. Policy Recommendations

Imagine for a moment that the Soviet Union had won the Cold War. Is it likely that globalization would have ever occurred? The model then would not have been one of a liberal political and economic system, but rather an imperial commonwealth in a spoke-and-wheel model. The benefits of such a system would not have flowed from the center to the periphery, but rather from the periphery to the imperial core. So, in a sense, globalization is the product not only of a unipolar, hegemonic world, but also of a particular kind of hegemon. It is the result of a particular set of structural conditions. This paper argues that globalization is an epiphenomenon of American hegemony, which gave it birth and sustains it through the political and economic institutions that govern the liberal international system. Globalization is a creature of US hegemony, informed by American political, cultural, and economic values, and will persist only as long as the United States remains the world's only superpower.

References

[1] US Department of Defense, http://beqiraj.com/usa/factsheets/navy/index.asp; R.J. Lieber, *The American Era* (New York: Cambridge University Press, 2005); and A.J. Bacevich, *The New American Militarism* (New York: Oxford University Press, 2005).

[2] See the World Bank, "World Development Indicators Database," August 2005; M. Mandelbaum, *The Case for Goliath: How America Acts as the World's Government in the Twenty-first Century* (New York: PublicAffairs, 2005); "A world empire by other means," *The Economist*, December 22, 2001.

[3] See D. Priest, *The Mission: Waging War and Keeping Peace with America's Military* (New York: W.W. Norton, 2003); *The Military Balance 2006* (London: IISS, 2006); *CIA World Factbook 2005,* see https://www.cia.gov/cia/publications/factbook/; and SIPRI data on World Military Expenditures 2005, see http://www.sipri.org/contents/milap/milex/mex_data_index.html.

[4] P. Kennedy, "The Greatest Superpower Ever," *New Perspectives Quarterly*, Winter 2002.

[5] See N. Ferguson, "Hegemony or Empire?," *Foreign Affairs*, September/October 2003; W.C. Wohlforth, "The Stability of a Unipolar World," *International Security*, Summer 1999.

[6] See M. Olson, *The Logic of Collective Action: Public Goods and the Theory of Groups* (Cambridge: Harvard University Press, 1965); C.P. Kindleberger, *The World in Depression, 1929-1939* (Berkeley: University of California Press, 1973); S.D. Krasner, "State Power and the Structure of International Trade," *World Politics*, April 1976; R. Gilpin, *US Power and the Multinational Corporation* (New York: Basic Books, 1975) and *War and Change in World Politics* (Cambridge: Cambridge University Press, 1981).

---

[7] See N.A. Graebner, *Foundations of American Foreign Policy* (Wilmington: Scholarly Resources, 1985); W.A. Williams, *From Colony to Empire: Essays in the history of American Foreign Relations* (New York: Wiley, 1972).

[8] See J. Kurth, "The Next NATO," *The National Interest*, Fall 2001.

[9] See R. Art, "Why Western Europe Needs the United States and NATO," *Political Science Quarterly*, Spring 1996; J. Joffe, "Europe's American Pacifier," *Foreign Policy,* Spring 1984; S. Huntington, "Why International Primacy Matters," *International Security*, Spring 1993; J. Nye, *Bound to Lead* (New York: Basic Books, 1990); R. Holbrooke, "America, A European Power," *Foreign Affairs*, March/April 1995.

[10] Quoted in Mandelbaum, *op. cit.*, note 2, pp. 95-96.

[11] See G. Bush and B. Scowcroft, *A World Transformed* (New York: Knopf, 1998); Vice President Cheney, Speech to Veterans of Foreign Wars, August 26, 2002; and especially Bacevich, *op. cit.*, note 1, pp. 179-201.

[12] Interview on *The Today Show*, February 19, 1998, available at http://secretary.state.gov/www/statements/1998/980219a.html.

[13] N. MacFarquhar, "Can't live with; Can't live without," *The New York Times,* January 16, 2005.

[14] See Lieber, *op. cit.*, note 1, pp. 4, 11, 53; Bacevich, *op. cit.*, note 1, pp. 83-93.

[15] See President Bush, State of the Union Address, January 31, 2006, available at http://www.whitehouse.gov/news/releases/2006/01/20060131-10.html.

[16] See C. Layne, "The Unipolar Illusion," *International Security*, Spring 1993.

[17] See Mandelbaum, *op. cit.*, note 2, pp. 172-175, 182-186.

[18] B.J. Cohen, "Containing Backlash: Foreign Economic Policy in an Age of Globalization," in R.J. Lieber (ed.), *Eagle Rules? Foreign Policy and American Primacy in the Twenty-First Century* (Upper Saddle River: Prentice Hall, 2002), p. 303.

CHAPTER 11

EDITORIAL OF POLICY BRIEF ON US HEGEMONY AND GLOBALIZATION

NAYEF R.F. AL-RODHAN

Dr. Nayef R.F. Al-Rodhan is Senior Scholar in Geostrategy and Director of the Program on the Geopolitical Implications of Globalization and Transnational Security at the Geneva Centre for Security Policy, Geneva, Switzerland

1. Review and Critique

With the demise of the bipolar system, the United States (US) is the only remaining superpower. Its global reach is such that François Heisbourg has referred to the US not simply as a superpower but as a "*hyperpuissance*."[1] With this unparalleled position comes heavy responsibilities, many of which the US has taken up. For example, the US played a pivotal role in the post-war reconstruction of Europe and the revival of world capitalism in the wake of the double shock of the Great Depression and World War II. The relative weakness of European countries as a result of economic devastation and the fragile position of their ruling classes made Western Europe's integration into an American-centered world order what Geir Lundestad has referred to as "empire by invitation."[2] In this context, the majority of Western European leaders were willing to accept American leadership. In return, as Mark Sheetz notes in his policy brief, the US provided an international financial and commercial order, as well as defense and security to its allies. The US has, in turn, benefited from this in that it has been able to impose its rules on the international system.[3]

A number of challenges to US hegemony have, nevertheless, begun to appear. The recovery of Western Europe and the rise of Japan as a formidable economic power put considerable pressure on the US position within the globalizing economy during the 1970s and 1980s. Nevertheless, the US managed to retain its position by virtue of the shift from the Bretton Woods system to a *de facto* pure dollar system,[4] which effectively allows the US to continue to maintain balance-of-payments deficits. Yet, the increased economic clout of China, in particular, is likely to become an increasing source of economic competition for the US. Thus, the temptation to opt for increased protectionism will be strong.

The legitimacy of US leadership is also being called into question. At the most benign level, Europeans are already pushing for greater autonomy in the Euro-Atlantic security realm. Their European Security and Defence Policy (ESDP), while still in its infancy, may increasingly erode the US monopoly on decision making within the Euro-Atlantic security arena.[5] Yet, a much more serious challenge to US leadership is being posed by the "empire's" discontents. How the US responds to this challenge will be crucial to its own stability and security, as well as to that of the rest of the world. Earlier, much of the strength of US hegemony lay in its democratic foundations and its capacity to act as a beacon of hope. This strength is, however, currently being undermined by US refusal to be restrained by international law and its abuse of human rights. Against the backdrop of diminishing credibility, the US risks embarking on what may be perceived as "empire by imposition." The Greater Middle Eastern Initiative, for example, is viewed by many in the region as pure imperialism. Thus, while the US is able to impose its will, doing so with disregard for international justice, as well as for foreign economic, political, and cultural traits, runs the risk of undermining US hegemony over the long term.

2. Dilemmas and Our Recommendations

In order for the United States to retain its leadership position and to promote greater stability and security across the globe, it must be a responsible hegemon. If it fails in this task, its long-term security, as well as the security of many people around the world, will be diminished. In what follows, we propose eight dilemmas or challenges facing the US and eight corresponding recommendations.

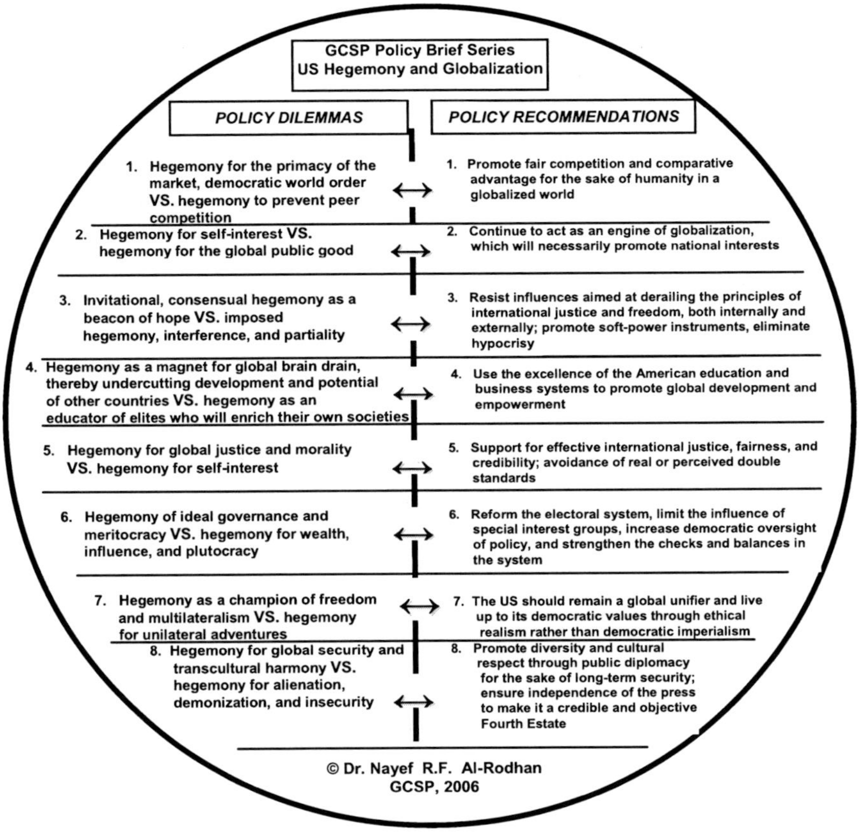

As mentioned, the post-World War II reconstruction of Europe was in many ways an example of invitational, consensual hegemony. European powers, for the most part, accepted US leadership against the backdrop of economic devastation, societal instability, and the Cold War. Yet, in other circumstances, US hegemony may, for real or perceived reasons, be viewed as outside interference or even outright imperialism. As a result, the US should resist derailing the principles of international justice and freedom, both internally and externally. It should also promote soft-power instruments and avoid hypocrisy.

Hegemony in a market democratic world is one thing; hegemony to prevent peer competition is another. For the sake of its long-term stability, the US should promote fair competition and comparative advantage for the sake of humanity in a globalized world. In order to be a "benevolent" hegemon, the US should continue to act as an engine of globalization, which will necessarily promote the national interest, but it should do so in a way that fosters greater economic justice within states, as well as between them. The US should also support effective international justice and fairness. Indeed, this will be a prerequisite for re-establishing its credibility.

As mentioned, the US has provided stability within the Euro-Atlantic area for the greater part of the post-World War II period. Within an altered security environment, the US now faces the choice of using its position to enhance global security and transcultural harmony or to demonize others, foster alienation, and generate increased insecurity. US policy makers should promote diversity and cultural respect through public diplomacy. Long-term stability and security are likely to depend on this. In the interest of preventing US misadventures, policy makers should also ensure the independence of the press domestically in order to make it a credible and objective Fourth Estate. This way, American voters might be in a better position to evaluate and criticize government decisions.

A large part of the explanation for US short-sightedness is linked to the power of special interests not only within the media but also within the political and electoral system. Ideally, the electoral system should be reformed in such a way as to limit the influence of special interest groups. In addition, democratic oversight, as well as checks and balances within the political system, should be augmented.

3. Conclusion

While affording a great deal of influence, US hegemony comes at a cost. In order to be durable, it must be responsible. In the interests of its own long-term stability and security, the US should take its responsibilities seriously. This implies underpinning its policies and actions with fairness, justice, and respect for other cultures. If the US fails to do this, it is likely not only to erode its dominant position but also to face increasingly difficult challenges at home and abroad.

References

[1] F. Heisbourg, "American Hegemony? Perceptions of the U.S. Abroad," *Survival*, Vol. 41, No. 4, 1999.

[2] G. Lundestad, "Empire by Invitation? The United States and Western Europe 1945-52," *Journal of Peace Research*, Vol. 23, No. 3, 1986.

[3] For the brief in its entirety, please see Chapter 10.

[4] P. Gowan, *The Global Gamble: Washington's Faustian Bid for World Dominance* (London and New York: Verso, 1999).

[5] L. Watanabe, "The ESDP: Between Estrangement and a New Partnership in Transatlantic Security Relations," *Journal of Contemporary European Studies*, Vol. 13, No. 1, 2005.

CHAPTER 12

DELIVERING REGIONAL SECURITY IN A GLOBALIZING WORLD: THE EUROPEAN UNION'S ENLARGEMENT TO TURKEY

ANNE DEIGHTON

Dr. Anne Deighton is Faculty Member at the Geneva Centre for Security Policy, Geneva, Switzerland and University Lecturer at the University of Oxford, United Kingdom

Abstract
The European Union is a vast and complex regional power center that delivers common rules and norms to its member states, and that is based on a mutual assumption of peace between its members.

European Union enlargement is an ongoing, voluntary, and proactive policy that contributes to regional and global security. The current challenges of enlargement are, nevertheless, considerable both for the Union and for Turkey.

Patient negotiations with Turkey must be considered a long-term, strategic security initiative that will, in the long run, strengthen the region and its borderlands, and create a win-win situation for both the Union and for Turkey.

1. Policy Challenges

In 2004, the European Union (EU) accepted 10 new states. This has taken its membership up from the original six members to 25. Some of the new member states were formerly part of the Soviet empire, and the enlargement negotiations were difficult and protracted. The anticipated admission of Bulgaria and Romania will also require careful consolidation. Many other states also wish to join the Union, while the prospect of Union membership has also been the greatest foreign policy tool for the EU in the Balkan region since the mid-1990s.

The challenge is to implement the promise of enlargement to Turkey, despite some hostility, so-called enlargement fatigue, and the competing foreign policy demands presented by the Balkan and Middle East regions.

2. Responses

The Union has been in enlargement negotiations with Turkey since October 2005 (Turkey signed an Association Agreement as long ago as 1963). All member states have agreed to the opening of negotiations, which are led by the European Commission. The enlargement package has to be agreed by Turkey as well as by all member states. The negotiations are difficult, given the enormity of the project: dossiers cover all aspects of political, social, and economic life, as well as related issues such as Cyprus. However, negotiating mechanisms are well established, given the last rounds of enlargement negotiations.

3. The dilemmas for the European Union

1. Turkey is vast: its territory is greater than that of any other single member state of the Union. It is anticipated that Turkey's population will be 80-85 million by 2026, whereas that of the Union's largest member state, Germany, will be only 80 million by then.

2. Turkey is poor, with about 35 percent of its population still employed in agriculture. Compared to the Union average of $28,000 per capita gross domestic product (GDP), that of Turkey is less than $7,000. Most of the immediate economic and investment benefits of enlargement have already been taken (as was the case with last enlargement), so there will be no immediate economic boom; instead, there will be high cohesion fund costs.

3. Turkey's accession would change the religious balance with the Union from roughly 3 percent Muslim to nearly 20 percent Muslim (Turkey is 99 percent Muslim).

4. Turkey's human rights record is improving, but the record in Turkey is still less than ideal over penal reform, rights for religious and racial minorities, and with regard to the influence of the military.

5. Turkey borders some very challenging countries. Its neighbors are Syria, Iraq, Iran, Armenia, Azerbaijan, Georgia, and Bulgaria, as well as Greece (a Union member).

6. Turkey is at the very center of a massive, cyclical, regional transformation. Nationalism; Kurdish issues; globalization and economic growth; religious questions; domestic political, social, and economic reform – in short, the heady mix of the politics of fear and of opportunity – jostle with each other for the attention of its citizens. Support for joining the Union appears high in Turkey, but the depth of that support is not really known.

7. Turkey's possible membership has always been a divisive issue within the Union. There has been considerable resistance in several parts of the Union to the application. This has come from countries and groups that – quite incorrectly – see Turkey as the "Other" and the Union as some kind of Christian club, as well as by those who fear uncontrolled immigration and the process of adaptation that they themselves will inevitably have to undergo to accommodate Turkey. Others fear that the Union would collapse administratively under the weight of Turkey's membership. There are also those who have some old historical scores to settle. There is talk of making a deal that would fall short of full membership, or of trying to sort out the Cyprus problem first.

Support seems to be slipping, as the Union deals with other issues, including globalization, the lack of a Union constitution, and security challenges in the Balkans and Middle East. The Cyprus question is both a divisive strategic issue and an accumulation of very difficult technical problems. It has been badly handled for many years and is currently proving to be a serious irritant in the enlargement application process.

Given this gloomy list, how can the Union both benefit from Turkey's membership and at the same time also deliver wider security?

1. Turkey has been a North Atlantic Treaty Organisation (NATO) member since 1952, and is exceptional in the Islamic world since its elites have taken a consistently clear, Westernizing path, broadly supporting the United States (US) despite recent tensions over the Iraq invasion. It is therefore already part of what is called the Western political security community. There is now no intrinsic conflict between membership in NATO and the EU, as this issue was dealt with in the last rounds of enlargement, and the US – the most important member of NATO – has been a consistent supporter of Union enlargement. Turkey, with its army of half a million, could make a substantial military contribution to the Union's common security and defense policies: as a NATO member, it has already contributed to military actions in the Balkans and Afghanistan.

2. If the conditions are right, there is no reason that the Union's single market could not support this expansion, even to the long-term extent of monetary union. Economists remain divided about optimal currency areas: the terrain is new and untested. Turkey is a young country, with 26 percent of its population under 15 years of age; as labor is going to be required inside the Union with its aging population, this will create a potential win-win situation. Its growth rates indicate its capacity to be a strong market, as well as a supplier of goods, labor, and services.

3. Turkey's geopolitical significance to the Balkans, the eastern Mediterranean, the Middle East, and the Russian region is self-evident. It has to look north, south, and east, as well as westward. It is, in every sense, a front-line state. It has sought to achieve a balance in its foreign policy priorities between the European Union and NATO, sustaining relations with Israel and Iran, as well as with its Arab neighbors, including Palestine. As a Mediterranean country, it has the capacity to

be a security provider with the EU in the region and to make an impact upon the EU's foreign policies.

4. Turkey's membership will represent the potential for a more confident and expansive European Union policy in the region: over time, Turkey should give capacity, local knowledge, and its foreign policy experience to the Union in one of the most important and rapidly changing regions of the world.

5. The Union is committed under its treaties to consider the application of a democratic country that respects the Union's fundamental democratic principles. It is clear that it will have to adapt its own working practices with this enlargement – but this is what the Union has always been able to do in the past.

6. Turkey is a secular state that has already made substantial and painful changes to its constitution and laws due to Union influence. The Union can use its leverage to embed these reforms into Turkish society. The application is being watched with interest in other parts of the Arab world as an example of how the Union manages relations with the Islamic world.

4. Implications

The implications are obvious enough: enlargement to Turkey is a long-term security policy that will nevertheless be difficult to achieve. The balance is between short-term fatigue, anxiety, and fear, and the long-term strategic and security interests of the Union. There is going to be resistance both within the Union and – if the negotiations are not carefully handled – also within Turkey.

(a) There are three possible scenarios

(i) Scenario 1

It would be a bleak scenario if the Union decided to pull back completely from its enlargement negotiations with Turkey, whether through a breakdown in negotiations or a negative vote or referendum in one of the existing member states.

1. Those same geopolitical strengths that Turkey's membership would bring could quickly turn to the Union's disadvantage: Turkey would be a rejected candidate, a member of NATO abandoned as a partner within the Union. Turkey could possibly look east, north, or south to reorient its foreign policies, and it would be under pressure to do so from nationalist groups in the country, although it is hard to see how exactly Turkey would find a new strategic role for itself. Turkey would still have four Union member states in its immediate vicinity, and it has been Greece that has successfully acknowledged the importance of enlargement for the two countries.

2. The Cyprus problem will not go away. It is not solely contingent upon Turkey's accession to the Union, and a diplomatic resolution is going to be essential, however delicate the issue.

3. Turkey's own domestic difficulties would be exacerbated, as its efforts to modernize and Westernize to make it an acceptable candidate could be lost. Its rapid economic growth would not be securely anchored in the Union framework, while its potentially unstable border and ethnic minority problems would certainly not be eased. Its efforts to deal with globalization and modernity within the perspective of Union membership would vanish.

4. The costs of non-membership would become increasingly unpleasant for the Union (as well as for Turkey) with every day that passes. To turn back from negotiations would be a major setback for both sides in an area of the world in which steady, multilateral progress is absolutely essential to stability.

5. The Union's own capacity to act in the Middle East would be severely constrained, as it would have essentially "opted out" of constructive engagement in the area, even if it offered long-term "association."

6. This would all reflect very badly upon the Union itself and would be far worse than having said, from the start, that

Turkey was not welcome in the Union club. A "No" would seem that the opportunities to create a vast and multicultural Union had been rejected in the face of fear: building a regional center in the face of globalization would have changed from an opportunity into a threat, with all the implications that Turkey has not been treated fairly because of its different racial and cultural mix.

(ii) Scenario 2

Too hasty an acceptance of Turkey's application – however improbable – would serve no good purpose, for whatever reason it was proposed, whether it was war, the complete collapse of Iraq, or greater instability in the Middle East. In the past, the Union has accepted member states before they were fully ready to meet the demands of membership: this generates ill feeling and destabilizes the functioning of the Union itself.

1. The Union has maximum leverage during the process of enlargement: conditionality is a powerful tool, as every negotiating team from the new member states would testify. This leverage also allows applicant states to carry out reforms that may cut deep into the grain of old traditions. All member states use the Union's demands as a rationale for carrying out sometimes unpopular changes, but this is even more strongly the case during an application negotiation. This process takes time, and needs time.

2. Likewise, enlargement is about adaptation and change management for civilians, both inside and outside the Union. Poor adaptation – as happened in the United Kingdom (UK), when the prospect of membership was badly presented to the British people – had long-term negative results for the Union and for the UK. The last enlargement has yet to be fully accommodated within the Union. In a globalizing world, time may always seem to be of the essence, but patience is necessary for people to adapt to major change.

(iii) Scenario 3

The most optimistic scenario is a long but constructive negotiation about Turkey's accession in which both parties learn to emphasize the positive over the negative, the opportunity over the threat.

1. The Union's foreign policy strategy is based upon the upgrading of common interests and a building of acceptance and partnership. This may sound whimsical – more Venus than Mars. But it is a misconception to imagine that this approach excludes toughness in negotiation, especially when issues that are central to the economy and civil life of a state, and to the good functioning of the Union, are at stake.

2. The negotiations will often be undertaken out of the public gaze. There may have to be side agreements on certain issues, perhaps relating to migration and a shifting of aid programs away from new members and toward Turkey. Practical prospects for dealing with drug trafficking and international crime can be addressed during the process of negotiation and then through membership. The hard bargaining that is led by the Commission will not stop until the necessary entry criteria have been achieved. Both sides will become increasingly locked in to the necessity of making the negotiation succeed.

3. There is a real challenge ahead to settle the issue of northern Cyprus, after the Commission was badly outmaneuvered in 2004 in a way that resulted in part of Cyprus joining the Union – with the full rights of veto upon subsequent enlargements. There is much diplomacy over Cyprus that will no doubt eventually require the continued input of many other international players.

4. However, although Turkish membership in the European Union does not represent the answer to the "clash of civilizations" issue, its long-standing membership in NATO and interest in membership in the Union make it a unique country in this part of the world. Further, although 90 percent Muslim, it is a secular, non-Arab state.

5. Both the Union and Turkey itself will be very different by the time – in at the very least a decade – that a unanimous decision has to be made on Turkey's membership. For the moment, the right principles have been established: pacific and voluntary enlargement in a setting that lays down clear basic norms, in the knowledge that this can bring strategic advantage to the Union in the Mediterranean and Middle Eastern region.

5. Policy Recommendations

1. ***Information*** Turkey is largely a closed book, except to specialists. Even those thousands of Union citizens who take their holidays in Turkey will know little of the country beyond the beaches and the bars. Likewise, it is not at all clear what kind of Union the citizens of Turkey think that they might be joining. Projects such as to propose that Istanbul be the culture capital of Europe in 2010 will clearly help. Discussions about Islam and the role of Islam in the state will help. The Commission will need to show the extent to which Turkey is modifying its constitution, improving its economic profile, and managing to bring its own people along in a massive process of modernization.

2. ***Mutuality*** means learning about Turkey and explaining ourselves. It means giving Turks the chance to reveal themselves and to learn about the Union and its member states. The place of enlargement in the life of the Union and the expectations of enlargement should be widely aired. Every enlargement has meant change for both applicants and the Union itself, and this will continue to be the case. The Union is a secular institution: its own institutional and decision-making problems can and will have to be fixed.

3. ***Education*** At a practical level, student exchanges at every level of the education system are one of the cheapest ways of educating the new elites about both the Union and about Turkey, and should be vigorously promoted by member states and the European Commission alike. This proposal should begin with universities and advanced technical and training

institutes: the cost of funding scholarships for visits, language teaching, and full educational programs for the rising elites is relatively very small.

Turkey should be high on the list of countries for student and staff exchanges, and for business and commercial meetings. Over the decade or so that the negotiations will take, a real qualitative impact could be made here.

4. ***Patience*** is needed, both from negotiators and from citizens. Some of the issues to be resolved are very tricky and involve entrenched interests, like Cyprus. Some, like dealing with the Armenian massacres of the early 20th century Ottoman Empire and similar episodes in history, are very emotive and require delicate handling and a high measure of honesty and humility from all. After all, the Union is already full of ex-imperial powers, none of which have a blemish-free past. The negotiators have to strike a balance between acknowledging Union reservations and driving forward on this major strategic project. In a globalizing world, issues of multicultural living and the acceptance that change cannot be avoided are now all part of the new rules of the game.

CHAPTER 13

EDITORIAL OF POLICY BRIEF ON DELIVERING REGIONAL SECURITY IN A GLOBALIZING WORLD: THE EUROPEAN UNION'S ENLARGEMENT TO TURKEY

NAYEF R.F. AL-RODHAN

Dr. Nayef R.F. Al-Rodhan is Senior Scholar in Geostrategy and Director of the Program on the Geopolitical Implications of Globalization and Transnational Security at the Geneva Centre for Security Policy, Geneva, Switzerland

1. Review and Critique

The enlargement of the European Union (EU) is a process that involves a complex set of agreements and requires the achievement of certain criteria (conditionality) before admittance. The unanimous agreement of all current members states is a hurdle that applicant states need to pass. In 2004, 10 new member states were admitted to the EU, fundamentally changing the character of the Union and increasing the complexity of its decision-making structures, given that 25 members are now sitting at the table.

Turkey's application to join the EU has arguably thus far stirred up the most debate among members. Supporters of Turkey's admission to the EU argue that the country is already a member of the security community, being a member and active contributor to the North Atlantic Treaty Organisation (NATO); that it is a secular and democratic state; and that it is an important contributor to peace and security in an otherwise volatile region (its border states include Iraq, Syria, and Iran, among others). Those skeptical and/or opposed to Turkey's admission point toward the size and population of the country, to its potentially unstable Islamic population, poor human rights record, lack of political stability, and neighboring countries. Fundamentally, opponents believe that "Europe's" border ends in the south east at Turkey, not beyond; proponents argue that Turkey is on the border and is historically an Islamic, Mediterranean, and European country.

Dr. Deighton's exploration of the issues involved in the EU's possible enlargement to Turkey, in the context of a globalizing world, highlights both of these sides and presents a number of possible scenarios for the next few years.[1] She particularly places the issue in a regional context, noting that Turkey is located in a rapidly changing region and one that is of great geopolitical importance. This in itself makes Turkey's accession to the EU particularly momentous. Dr. Deighton envisages three possible scenarios: (1) an end to negotiations, due, for example, to eroding support in member states; (2) a precipitate acceptance of Turkey to the EU or, most optimistically she notes; (3) a lengthy and constructive negotiation process that allows Turkey and the EU member states to develop a greater understanding of each other.

The issue is not simple, and its complexity is marked by the sectors that Dr. Deighton's brief explores – political, security, social, economic, etc. – and the position that vested, fixed ideas on debates between West and East, Christianity and Islam have on this enlargement debate. It should not be taken for granted that the Turkish population supports its country's membership in the EU. The EU remains an attractive "club" for the political establishment as well, but this could always change. Dr. Deighton's recommendations reflect the need for greater exchange of information, especially at the grassroots level, and understanding between the actors involved. Of course, it should not be forgotten that, while recognizing the importance of these aspects, they must be accompanied by concerted change at the political and economic levels.

2. Dilemmas and Our Recommendations

The dilemmas inherent in Turkey's application to join the European Union are multifaceted and evoke a number of themes and topics: religion, economic disparity, and ideas on what "Europe" actually is, which are illustrative of broader dilemmas facing the European Union today. The EU and Turkey face a difficult path in reconciling respective interests, finding a balance on the achievement of practical measures (economic, social, and political), and, of course, also on a more emotional level. The eight dilemmas and corresponding recommendations below reflect these aspects and present concrete options for increasing mutual understanding.

Each of the above pairs is important in its own right; however, for ease of analysis only a few will be discussed, evoking some of the broader themes.

First, the issue underlying Turkey's potential accession is related to the EU's own internal problems following a major enlargement in 2004. Turkey's accession process has been wrapped up with these bureaucratic issues, and admittedly a form of identity crisis of the Union itself. A longer accession process will be one way to handle any major negative impact.

Second, Turkey's possible entry into the EU needs to be viewed from the point of view of potential benefits. Turkey's young population can remedy labor shortages in the EU, and a robust Turkish economy in certain areas can be an asset to the European community. The country has made important contributions to NATO, and its experience in this multilateral forum should not be discounted. In addition, the importance of its location cannot be ignored, and its role as a regional force contributing to peace and cooperation in its neighborhood is a significant factor and something that will potentially multiply in effect if it becomes a member of the EU.

Third, promoting cross-cultural understanding among the populations of the EU and Turkey will produce important mid- to long-term results. Ignorance and a lack of understanding promote prejudices that will work against both Turkish and EU interests. Programs that encourage and support educational exchanges, as noted by Dr. Deighton, are one example of activities that could promote mutual understanding. Public information campaigns in EU member states on Turkey's political, social, and religious character and in Turkey concerning the EU accession process can only have a positive effect.

3. Conclusion

Given the complexity of the issues involved surrounding Turkey's possible accession to the EU, it is not possible to recommend one or two things that will for certain change the situation dramatically in the short term. Concerns surrounding Turkey's membership application to the EU stem from a certain degree of misunderstanding but also from genuine worries over an ever-decreasing effectiveness of an ever-enlarging Union and the number of outstanding requirements the country needs to fulfill before membership. Although these concerns are warranted, they need to be carefully weighed against the benefits of Turkey's accession as outlined above. The process of possibly admitting Turkey to the Union, which is already under way, will not be undertaken with haste, nor should it be. The process of democratic, economic, and social change in Turkey has already made significant gains, but it needs to continue. The full support of Turkey's population and of EU entities and members states is a crucial factor in making the possible future accession of Turkey to the European Union more than just a success but also an opportunity to bridge cultural divides and dispel broader misconceptions.

References

[1] For the brief in its entirety, please see Chapter 12.

CHAPTER 14

ETHICS, CIVIL LIBERTIES, GLOBALIZATION, AND GLOBAL SECURITY

ANDREAS BUSCH

Dr. Andreas Busch is Reader in European Politics at the University of Oxford, United Kingdom

Abstract
This paper aims to provide the reader with a structured discussion of the issue of global security challenges caused by transnational terrorism, with a focus on the ethical and civil liberties challenges posed by governmental efforts to fight terrorism. It does so by first detailing the policy challenges in this area, then tracing state responses to these challenges, and analyzing the dilemmas and implications inherent in these responses. The paper then proceeds to sketch future scenarios before arriving at some policy recommendations.

1. Policy Challenges

The terrorist attacks on the United States (US) on September 11, 2001 put the issue of transnational terrorism on center stage. This event, which dramatically increased awareness of transnational terrorism as a threat to global security, was a transformative event in world politics. The attacks in Bali, Madrid, and London in the years since have reinforced that development.

Terrorism, for many countries, is not new – domestic terrorism of a nationalist or ideological nature has been around for decades in countries such the United Kingdom (IRA), Spain (ETA), Germany (Red Army Faction) or Italy (Brigate Rosse). While varying in intensity over time, this kind of terrorism tended to work by targeting representatives of society's elite, thus avoiding major civilian casualties. Government responses were firm but focused in order to avoid promoting popular support for the terrorist causes through excessive repression. Today's transnational terrorism, however, is different from domestic terrorism in a number of ways. First, it is literally global in nature, striking on different continents. Second, its main means is indiscriminate mass killing of civilians and the spread of fear; today's terrorist acts are not designed to inspire support for any specific goal. Finally, responses to terrorist acts have taken place both on the national level (e.g., new anti-terrorism legislation) and the international level (e.g., warfare against states suspected of harboring terrorists and facilitating their actions).

Although transnational terrorism by itself is a manifest challenge, its effect has been exacerbated by the changing nature of the international political system over the course of recent decades. Scholars have talked of "post-international politics," emphasizing that more and more of the actions that sustain world politics unfold without the direct involvement of nations or states. In contrast to the international system of the Cold War era, no clear "blocs" facing each other exist today. In addition, European-inspired concepts such as sovereignty and territoriality are in decline while identity issues are on the rise, as are "sovereignty free actors," ranging from non-governmental organizations like Greenpeace all the way to Al-Qaida. Attempts to analyze this situation on a theoretical level have used metaphors such as "turbulence" and have likened the new complexities in the international political universe to those of the pre-state world by speaking of a "New Middle Age." States, thus, face a situation in which the distinction between foreign and domestic events is fading, while states' capacity to act against threats of a transnational nature is declining. Transnational terrorism is, thus, a consequence rather than a cause of the weakening of state power.

Further compounding the challenge is the fact that in many countries – especially in Continental Europe – governments are increasingly faced with popular demands for an "ethical foreign policy" and the desire to reject or at least minimize the use of armed force as a tool in the foreign policy arsenal; these attitudes further weaken governments' capacity to respond to threats from abroad.

2. Responses

If states have in many ways been weakened by the developments of the last two decades, it might seem paradoxical that the initial consequence of transnational terrorism has been a reassertion of statehood in many countries. This has been the case in three dimensions:

Strengthening territoriality

Under the heading of "homeland security," many countries have massively increased the resources devoted to protection of their territory, often employing sophisticated new technologies such as radiation detection or the use of military hardware. In addition, comprehensive, often voluminous laws (such as the "USA PATRIOT Act," the "Anti-Terrorism, Crime and Security Emergency Bill 2001" in the United Kingdom (UK) and similar laws in France and Germany) have given the executive a host of new powers, while organizational reforms have often lowered or torn down established "Chinese walls" between police and intelligence services.

Protection against foreigners

Since the threat is almost universally perceived to come from outside, immigration controls have been stepped up and many countries have phased in a new requirement for biometric passports for foreign visitors. Even resident foreigners are now faced with new powers of deportation and extradition, many of which have no or only poor standards of judicial or constitutional review.

Waging war

States that have provided transnational terrorists with operational bases (such as Afghanistan) or have been accused of doing so (such as Iraq) have found themselves under attack by varying coalitions operating under the leadership of the United States. Fought under the label of a "war on terror," these wars have had a an ultimate objective that stretched beyond defeat to "regime change" and "democratization." Further, since combatants were often not organized in conventional armies, they were often denied normal treatment under the Geneva Conventions and interned in places such as the (constitutionally extraterritorial) US detention facility at Guantánamo Bay.

To date, these measures have been of a conventional quality – most of them stem from a standard policy repertoire that has not (yet?) been adapted to the new quality of the threat. This is likely to at least contribute to the dubious effectiveness of many of these measures so far.

One example is the constantly declining success of the war in Iraq, which has left the country sliding towards full-blown civil war. Combined with the illegitimacy of the war under international law, the humanitarian debacle in Iraq has substantially undermined support for the intervention in most states belonging to the Iraq war coalition, including the US and the UK.

And while police and intelligence services claim to have thwarted some planned further attacks (but for obvious reasons can give no detailed information), no feeling of safety or resolution of conflict has been established by enacting the new legislation. Rather, the emergence of "home grown" terrorists (most clearly in the case of the United Kingdom) has deepened the sense of insecurity among the populace. Furthermore, analysis of the anti-terrorism legislation shows it to be largely ineffective: in the UK, for example, of the 895 persons arrested under the Terrorism Act 2000, only 23 were convicted.

3. Dilemmas

Policy makers face a number of substantial dilemmas in taking action against transnational terrorism. One is concerned with the public sphere: while politicians need to be seen as taking firm action in the face of security threats, the consequences of overzealous or inept enforcement of these policies – and even the policies themselves – may well endanger fundamental civil liberties and thus undermine public support for the policies and policy makers. This is true for both the domestic and international spheres.

The dilemma of weakening the traditional liberal values of Western democracies as part of an attempt to defend them is also a very serious one. As an abstract point, it is quite evident that bypassing standard democratic oversight rules in order to ultimately defend those same rules is not a convincing attitude in the long run. As the discussions about indefinite detention without charge and extraordinary rendition have shown, many politicians and legal systems, nevertheless, seem to have chosen to follow a more short-term oriented calculus.

It is also clear in the abstract that no liberal state can provide complete security and that any attempt to do so would endanger the rule of law, because any state that truly maximizes security would have to develop totalitarian features. On the other hand, measures such as the retention of telecommunications data (which civil liberties groups argue undermine data protection regulations) have proved effective in the prevention of terrorist acts or the tracking down of culprits after a terrorist act has taken place.

It is, however, unclear, against whom efforts to solve the terrorism threat should be directed. The initial response, to see transnational terrorism as a threat from outside (implying that all citizens are loyal anyway and conventional measures – as outlined above – will be effective), has been exposed as fallacious by the London bombings of July 7, 2005. This further emphasizes that transnational terrorism is substantively a battle of values, which cannot ultimately be won by force.

4. Implications

Public debates about states' reactions to transnational terrorism are, therefore, of the utmost importance; to date, they have been very fierce. The following quotations from the United States and the United Kingdom may serve to illustrate these antagonistic viewpoints:

- "To those who scare peace-loving people with phantoms of lost liberty, my message is this: Your tactics only aid terrorists, for they erode our national security and diminish our resolve." (US Attorney General John Ashcroft)

- "Since September 11, the government has enacted legislation, adopted policies, and threatened procedures that are not consistent with our established laws and values and would have been unthinkable before." (US legal scholar Ronald Dworkin)

- "The most important liberty is that of harm from others." (UK Prime Minister Tony Blair)

- "Indefinite imprisonment in consequence of a denunciation on grounds that are not disclosed and made by a person whose

> identity cannot be disclosed is the stuff of nightmares, associated whether accurately or inaccurately with France before and during the Revolution, with Soviet Russia in the Stalinist era and now associated, as a result of section 23 of the 2001 Act, with the United Kingdom." (UK Law Lord, Lord Scott)

What is clearly at issue is the extent to which civil liberties can be infringed, with the ultimate stated goal of protecting those same liberties. In the "war on terror," prisoner abuse in the Abu Ghraib prison in Baghdad, detention at Camp X-Ray in Guantánamo Bay without recourse to legal protection, and Central Intelligence Agency (CIA) flights involving "extraordinary rendition" (even of European citizens), and secret prisons have undermined the legitimacy of state action and have damaged the goal of winning "hearts and minds" at least as much as the lack of decisive military success.

The debate on torture is a particular case in point. One side argues that the "war on terror" requires extraordinary measures and that "highly coercive interrogation" is justified, given the duty to protect potential victims and the impossibility of deterring, for example, suicide bombers by conventional means. Others point to the fact that breaking legal obligations (such as the Universal Declaration of Human Rights) and stretching the definition of torture to serve a current purpose is deeply alien to liberal values, will result in severe harm to the institutions of liberal democracy (and their appeal abroad), and that information obtained through such measures is of dubious value not only morally, but also factually.

In a world of globalized communication and migration, the battle for "hearts and minds" is one that has to be conducted both domestically and abroad. Many societies will therefore have to step up their efforts at internal integration. Especially in Europe, the estimated 15 million Muslim residents have been "living together separately" rather than being integrated socially and politically. In the past, debates in these societies have failed to fully appreciate the necessary consequences of allowing large numbers of immigrants to enter their countries, not only in terms of granting immigrants citizenship and rights to full political participation, but also in demanding that immigrants accept their new countries' liberal values. After a long period of delay, the present confrontations may serve as a wake-up call, but how societies will react to that is far from certain.

Lastly, it has to be said that the "war on terror" is being used opportunistically by authoritarian countries as an excuse to crack down on their domestic political opponents, separatists, and religious groups. Cases in point include Belarus, China, Egypt, Russia, Syria, and Zimbabwe. This only further serves to emphasize how important it is for Western countries to uphold their liberal values in the process of defending them.

5. Future Trajectories/Scenarios

A positive scenario for the future is one that avoids confrontation by emphasizing the use of diplomacy over force, concentrates on winning of "hearts and minds," builds a far-ranging coalition against transnational terrorism and expects medium- to long-term positive results. This position draws on the experience of the Cold War confrontation in Europe, the positive effects of the dialogue-centered "Ostpolitik" and the successful stabilization and transformation of transition countries in Central and Eastern Europe. This position encourages those seeking "regime change" to pursue this goal mainly through peaceful means. It is questionable, however, whether the same approach can really be adapted to a non-territorial threat.

Conversely, a negative scenario would emphasize the use of power, the capacity to mobilize unparalleled forces, and the ability to strike anywhere on the globe. This position also draws on the Cold War experience, but with a different viewpoint, namely that of outspending the Soviet Union into collapse. It also includes the option of armed "regime change" and the requirement for swiftly changing coalition partners; this approach risks antagonizing countries whose cooperation might be important for victory over transnational terrorism (e.g., Saudi Arabia and Pakistan). In addition to involving huge costs, it is even more unclear whether such a strategy would work in a de-territorialized conflict, and whether or not it might have adverse effects by providing transnational terrorism with a heroic narrative, both for their fighters and the wider global public (see the experiences of Vietnam).

A third scenario then seems most likely, namely that of an unsystematic mix of both strategies, primarily because the multitude of actors involved is unlikely to agree on very much and thus will adopt different strategies, even though this will weaken their overall effectiveness and undermine their political stance. National and ideological preferences as well as varying political calculations will contribute to this. An increased involvement of international organizations, however, could provide some coordination.

6. Policy Recommendations

President Bush's declaration of the "war on terror" with the famous statement "either you're with us, or you're with the terrorists" leaves no space for those disagreeing with the strategies and tactics adopted by either side. Such a binary, Manichaean distinction is also ill-suited to constructive political discourse and thus runs counter to the very essence of liberal democracy it seeks to defend. As a consequence, the effort has become increasingly unpopular in many countries; even in the United States, many of the powers assumed by the President (such as convening military tribunals for non-citizen terrorist suspects without a formal declaration of war) are being challenged in the courts.

The amorphous nature of the opponent and the undefined goal of the "war on terror" means that it has achieved little visible success and is unlikely to come to a clear conclusion in the foreseeable future. Opposition is therefore likely to rise in many liberal democracies, while the popularity of the transnational terrorism cause may broaden in many other countries, particularly if other groups (be they separatist, ideological or anti-globalization) manage to link their specific concerns to it.

But countries can and must respond to these challenges. Measures need to be taken on both the domestic and the international level:

1. **Domestically, countries have to practice what they preach in order to be credible.** Opting out of Human Rights Conventions, suspending due process, and applying highly questionable measures such as indefinite detention and extraordinary rendition will ultimately hurt Western liberal democracies' cause against transnational terrorism both domestically and abroad.

2. **Politicians should be frank that there is no quick comprehensive fix to the threats posed by transnational terrorism.** While it has to be acknowledged that elected

officials and policy makers are under short-term pressures, with voters expecting them to take action and succeed in protecting the populace, only a viable long-term strategy will ultimately increase security for their societies. The problem is thus one of time horizons. It may provide some consolation to consider that, objectively, transnational terrorism has not been a substantial cause of casualties so far (about 4000 victims in five years, with the vast majority incurred on 9/11).

3. **Societal discourse about the advantages of liberal democracy must be encouraged, for it will strengthen resolve against transnational terrorism in the case of an attack.** In a globalized world, many societies have become less homogeneous through immigration; acknowledging this fact and addressing it constructively will go a long way towards better integrating society. Studying the institutional solutions by which previously deeply divided societies have successfully overcome their tensions (e.g., adopting consociational strategies and institutions) may also be helpful in this respect.

4. **On the international level, opportunities for cooperation within the framework of the United Nations must be used to coordinate national strategies.** The new Human Rights Council could be one forum for this, but the current US administration's opposition to it (as its lack of recognition of the International Criminal Court and its skepticism towards multilateralism in general) puts a serious damper on prospects for this. The planned UN Peacebuilding Commission may help find ways to support post-conflict reconstruction efforts and, thus, stop countries from turning into failing states that can become havens for transnational terrorism. It would seem only appropriate for a quintessentially global problem to be addressed in a global forum.

CHAPTER 15

EDITORIAL OF POLICY BRIEF ON ETHICS, CIVIL LIBERTIES, GLOBALIZATION, AND GLOBAL SECURITY

NAYEF R.F. AL-RODHAN

Dr. Nayef R.F. Al-Rodhan is Senior Scholar in Geostrategy and Director of the Program on the Geopolitical Implications of Globalization and Transnational Security at the Geneva Centre for Security Policy, Geneva, Switzerland

1. Review and Critique

Since it became known that the United States (US) National Security Agency (NSA) was monitoring both US citizens and communications with individuals from around the world in order to better prepare themselves for future attacks in the "war on terror,"[1] the world has re-focused itself on the debates between civil liberties, ethics, and transnational security. At what level can states monitor citizens within its own borders? What types of information are they able to acquire and hold about their own citizens residing in other countries as well as individuals communicating with contacts in the US, regardless of their country of origin? The debate stems from the role that various legal institutions must play in these circumstances and where governments must be accountable for the level of surveillance that they pursue in their quest for national security.[2]

While this issue can be understood in a number of contexts, it has been raised most recently due to the global war on terror. Dr. Andreas Busch[3] centers his arguments, therefore, quite correctly, around this very issue. As Dr. Busch notes, governmental justification for this level of monitoring stems directly from the type of threat that transnational terrorism poses. It is not a threat that is concentrated in its targets; rather, it is very global in its reach and target zones, making it very difficult to track. In addition, transnational terrorists aim to spread fear through civilian populations by indiscriminately targeting them in their daily lives. Consequently, responses have developed both on the national and international levels.[4]

It is, therefore, not surprising that a number of policy dilemmas have surfaced at the state level. Although it has always been critical for states to monitor the activities of proven or potential criminals discreetly, today's issues center around governments (in this case the US, although it is not the only country to implement these types of measures) avoiding proper judicial oversight channels, excusing their flouting of law with claims of new executive powers and unprecedented requirements for speed and efficiency. The Bush administration, by ordering these surveillance techniques, overstepped the legal requirements of the Foreign Intelligence Surveillance Act (FISA) of 1978, which was designed to protect citizens from unlawful warrantless surveillance.[5] Despite laws such as FISA, in reality, the current *modus operandi* of some governments, particularly the US, in this case, has been to arrest individuals who fall largely under the prosecution threshold. Consequently, these individuals find themselves under arrest in places such as the detention facility in Guantánamo Bay, Cuba, without a constitutionally-mandated due process, such as being officially charged with a crime or being given access to legal representation.

The resulting questions center around what type of operations governments should be allowed to conduct in this manner and under what conditions and with what judicial oversight exceptions should be allowed. How should states be held accountable when they cross the line? To what authoritative body or bodies should states be accountable and from whence will the support (both financial and political legitimacy) for these bodies be derived?

2. Dilemmas and Our Recommendations

It is important to note that in the development of these dilemmas and recommendations, some of the seeming dilemmas may not appear as such. In fact, part of what makes each of these dilemmas gain such a status is the way that the problem is perceived and, therefore, handled in the state apparatus, rather than through the presented statement itself. Keeping this point in mind, we present the following challenges and recommendations as the means for states to pursue their national security objectives, but in a way that preserves basic liberties and civil rights.

The protection of the state versus the protection of the individual is a dilemma which has been more recently debated, also in terms of civil liberties and ethics. The term "ethical states" seems like a concept that could never be used in today's modern discourse. However, it is a concept and a norm that is vital and must be maintained if there is to be credible stability and security within the international system.

In most cases, elected officials and policy makers would like to protect their populace and democracies. Too often, initial attempts to protect the populace are not well thought out; over-reactions, scapegoating and anti-democratic, "quick fix" approaches are not uncommon in a state that perceives itself as under attack. Unfortunately, this is costly in terms of democratic values in a pluralistic society. This also becomes problematic when political leaders would like to (or have to) identify various suspects and maintain this group without subjecting large numbers of people from being alienated, tracked unnecessarily, and treated as suspect, purely on the basis of their appearance, culture, ethnicity, or religious affiliation. The state has at all times a clear responsibility to protect the larger, unfairly targeted group, despite the possibility that a small minority of criminal suspects may hide within this larger but innocent group.

Human security must take precedence at every level, because without security on the individual level, there can never be true state security, at least not in a democratic state. States should encourage and therefore promote integration and transnational and transcultural cooperation. This could be supported by respectful and inclusive political statements on the part of the state. Statements such as, "If you are not with us, then you are with the terrorists"[6] do little to promote further cooperative efforts toward understanding. The state should encourage assimilation of these groups and cooperative efforts at the local level within the relevant communities.

Naturally, there are times when a state has correctly identified a suspect and consequently needs to monitor activities in order to document and, one hopes, prevent potential or actual criminal activity. There is certainly justification at this juncture for surveillance and the creation of watch lists. However, there should be a legal check of all of these activities. Security services should be monitored and must be required to adhere to strict oversight regulations in order to ensure that fair and legal processes are reliably practiced.

Another looming problem for states has been the accuracy of their watch lists and the resources required to properly maintain them. This requires that states must consistently and constantly update and verify their lists in order to ensure that these lists remain accurate.[7] States must also provide mechanisms that innocent citizens mistakenly placed on these lists may use to refute false or mistaken claims against them and regain their right to travel without needless harassment, unnecessary delays, and embarrassment.

While the prisoners in the detention facility in Guantánamo await their day in court, legal experts outside Cuba have adamantly opposed the Bush administration's designation of these prisoners as "enemy combatants" rather than prisoners of war. There is also much consternation about long detentions without, in many cases, any official charges or access to an attorney. While it is understood that these cases quite often involve individuals whose lives are at stake should they provide critical information for the prosecution, it does not eliminate the constitutional requirement for due process or excuse the need for the government to use proper judicial channels and procedures. Timely and special courts (provided that they are still monitored properly) should be created to ensure secrecy where necessary, but these courts should also guarantee legality and impartiality. No state is above the widely accepted international norms and conventions; it is imperative that each state vigorously apply, without exception, these standards in order to ensure the civil liberties and human rights of all individuals.

The state has an important role to play in providing security to its populace, but it must be regulated to ensure that the state itself does not become a threat. Responsible and thorough educational systems, responsible and accountable media services, and inclusive political statements should work to separate the guilty few from the innocent majorities. When the line between a possibly guilty minority and an innocent majority becomes blurred due to a lack of clarity on the part of the state system, a dangerous situation develops. Instead of targeting all individuals in an ethnic or religious group that may indeed contain legitimate criminal suspects, the state should encourage acceptance, tolerance, and assimilation of that group into the larger population. In so doing, the state increases its ability to enlist that community's cooperation in keeping its members law abiding. The objective of such efforts should be to engender the new group's loyalty to its host country. Unless efforts to simultaneously promote assimilation and decrease alienation are undertaken, it becomes more difficult to separate those who wish no harm to the state from those that are potentially and actually dangerous.

3. Conclusion

Today, perhaps more than at any time in decades, states still find it difficult to properly balance required civil liberties and ethics against national and international security; too often, these concepts appear to exist in competition with one another. Policy makers and state officials must work harder to maintain those liberties that democratic societies hold in such high esteem in order to maintain the hearts of the people. Once people feel that even their own states consider them to be suspects – suspects no longer able to expect the due process required by their own country's laws and constitution – that state has started to slide down a slippery slope, a tendency that will be difficult to reverse. States must incorporate discipline into their systems and enforce rigorous checks and balances of each sector of their governmental apparatus in order to ensure security on all levels. Security checks and guarantees must also occur for those citizens who wish to visit certain countries; random checks should only be conducted fairly and respectfully, when appropriate. When this is required, states should maintain a professionalism and a level of respect that is in conjunction with international norms and conventions. This way, states will build the respect and trust of those living within their borders and therefore work towards an even greater level of security along with the protection of civil liberties for all law-abiding citizens.

References

[1] For a look at the debates surrounding the leak of the NSA program and the Bush administration involvement, please see http://www.cnn.com/2005/POLITICS/12/17/bush.nsa/ in addition to the related articles also listed.

[2] This became a public debate when it was revealed that President Bush had authorized the unwarranted monitoring of citizens shortly after September 11, 2001. For more information, please see J. Risen and E. Lichtblau, "Bush Lets U.S. Spy on Callers Without Courts," *The New York Times*, December 16, 2005, http://www.nytimes.com/2005/12/16/politics/16program.html?ei=5090&en=e32072d786623ac1&ex=1292389200.

[3] For the brief in its entirety, please see Chapter 14.

[4] *Ibid.*, these arguments also appear in this publication by A. Busch.

[5] For a review of FISA and the way in which the Bush administration has operated its wiretapping without warrants, including the justification for doing so, please see, "National Security Department: Listening In," *The New Yorker,* "Talk of the Town," May 22, 2006, at http://www.newyorker.com/talk/content/articles/060529ta_talk_hersh.

[6] See "Address to a Joint Session of Congress and the American People – President Declares 'Freedom at War with Fear'," September 20, 2001, http://www.whitehouse.gov/news/releases/2001/09/20010920-8.html.

[7] In 2004, innocent individuals were detained as a result of their names appearing on terror watch lists as they tried to enter the United States, raising concerns about these lists and their accuracy. See G. Taylor, "U.S. Terror Watch List Keeps Eyes on All Groups," *The Washington Times*, February 22, 2004, http://www.washingtontimes.com/national/20040222-122717-6118r.htm.

CHAPTER 16

INFORMAL REMITTANCE FLOWS AND THEIR IMPLICATIONS FOR GLOBAL SECURITY

MIRIAM AHMED FUGFUGOSH

Ms. Miriam Ahmed Fugfugosh is Course Coordinator for the European Training Course in Security Policy and Exercises and Skill Development Training Officer at the Geneva Centre for Security Policy, Geneva, Switzerland

Abstract

Remittances, an inextricable facet of migration, are the sums of money that migrants regularly, usually monthly, send home to their families who have remained in their countries of origin. Recipients spend these funds in various ways: for some, remittances are their lifeline, without which they do not eat, as in Somalia; for others, remittances are transferred home specifically to be invested in savings schemes with attractive incentives, as in India. In Cape Verde, migrant remittances contributed to political change of the oppressive island government while for people from other countries, remittances are directed to community infrastructure development, such as collective projects in Mexico. These illustrations convey the message that in all corners of the globe, remittances are a precious tool for every single recipient and that the secure flow of remittances must be assured. It is essential for the international community to grasp that it is the poorest and most vulnerable individuals who are strikingly impacted by remittances, positively by their receipt, but devastatingly by their cessation. Overwhelmingly, it is this latter population who employs a method of remittance transfer susceptible to criminal abuse, which consequently poses a possible threat to the international community. The dichotomy of this security dilemma is challenging the well-being of a gamut of actors and begs a solution.

1. The Policy Challenge

(a) The Weight of Remittance Flows

In 2005, migrant remittances were estimated to be $167 billion, more than twice the size of international aid flows. The actual size of remittances remains unknown due to the lack of a common international classification for the funds, in addition to information gaps from the informal sector. "There is no universal agreement yet on how to measure international migrants' remittances," however the calculation usually includes "'workers' remittances, compensation of employees, and migrant transfers."[1] Were precise data known, the World Bank predicts that the value of remittances could in fact increase by 50 percent or more.[2]

Remittance flows have risen 73 percent in the last five years.[3] This is due to many factors, one being that migration has undergone a metamorphosis. Not only have migration rates doubled since 1980, which implicitly increases workers' remittances, but the way people migrate has changed.[4] Circular, or temporary, migration is now more common than permanent emigration. In addition, contact and involvement with families in countries of origin are solidly maintained; individuals sent abroad to countries where earnings are higher are considered investments for the benefit of the entire family. These migrants remit a portion of their wages to their families at home out of a sense of moral responsibility and duty. Estimated per capita remittances to Africa from family members residing in developed countries is approximated at $200 per month[5] – a significant amount when contrasted with the average $2 per day earnings of individuals in many developing nations. Improved data collection, driven by greater awareness of the development potential of remittances, as well as heightened concerns about possible money laundering and terrorist financing explains this reported increase in remittances.

(b) The Uses and Usefulness of Remittances

The World Bank states that "international remittances accounted for 60 percent of income for households in the lowest income decile."[6] In such impoverished homes, remittances primarily pay for food, health services, and education, the last of which has a direct influence on girls, for whom school is often a luxury. In all contexts, remittances diversify household economies, reducing risk for families, enlarging disposable income, and allowing for investment in new opportunities, such as small businesses and savings. In Africa, remittances are more likely to reach poverty-stricken homes than other sources of capital or aid.[7] In failed states, such as Somalia, without banking structures, remittances remain the most reliable source of income distributed among relatives; "a 63 year-old grandmother…told IRIN she and 12 members of her extended family were living on the $150 a month one of her sons remitted to Somalia each month."[8] Remittances also lessen the severity of traumatic aftermaths of natural disasters as well as periods of financial volatility and government instability; they have increased after recent humanitarian disasters, including the Asian financial crisis, the 2004 tsunami, and the collapse of the Somali state, preventing victims from feeling the full depth of despair. Although the impact of remittances is most striking on transient poverty, if harnessed properly, the long term benefit potential could represent significant contributions to development and enduring poverty reduction.

(c) The *Hawala* System: A Source of Insecurity?

There are various systems through which remittances are transferred about the world. For the purposes of this brief, it is sufficient to stress that systems are either formal (Western Union or banks, for example) or informal systems, known as *hawalas*. *Hawala* is an informal banking system in which funds are transferred internationally, without being moved physically. *Hawala* brokers, whose relationships are based in part on trust, maintain running accounts with one another. Once a sender deposits funds with a *hawala* broker, the broker contacts another *hawala* broker in the relevant location and requests the dispersal of funds to the recipient. *Hawala* brokers employ fast methods of communication, such as phone or fax. The main users of the *hawala* system reside in the developed world and transfer funds to recipients in the developing world. Users include migrant workers, who regularly send a portion of their earnings home to their families, and families established in the West, who support relatives in their home country.

It is this informal *hawala* system that is feared by governments because of the lacuna of information it creates as a result of its informal nature and minimal documentation. *Hawala* brokers maintain running accounts with one another; a phone call, fax, or email suffices for a disbursement of hundreds of dollars to a recipient. In the *hawala* system, however, the money is transferred without being physically moved, taken from pools of funds kept by each broker. Personal relationships contribute to the reliability and the success of the *hawala* system. Some argue that "these transfer houses know their customers better than formal banks as the service works entirely on trust, through clan and kinship arrangements."[9]

Hawala is appealing to migrants for many reasons. Less expensive than formal transfer methods, *hawala* fees can be as low as 1 to 5 percent compared to possible excesses of 20 percent in formal channels, although fees usually remain around 10 to 15 percent.[10] As opposed to commercial banks, *hawala* generates minimal documentation; this is often preferred by migrants intimidated by the extensive bureaucracy of the formal system (this tends to be especially true for individuals with questionable visa status). Furthermore, any paper trail is generally destroyed once the recipient has collected the promised sum, thus offering senders a certain anonymity. Finally, *hawala* transfers remain fast, generally quicker than any official system, so funds can be collected by recipients in as little as two hours.[11] This system is used by people around the globe; it is important to note however, that while some users have other options, such as other transfer companies with whom to do business, there are many people in some parts of the world who have absolutely no option beside *hawalas*.

The policy challenge put forth is the improvement of all aspects of security surrounding remittance flows, both formal and informal. However, special attention must be directed towards the informal channels, as their users are generally the most vulnerable. Improving the security of the *hawala* system is undeniably crucial for the well-being of the entire international community, from individual states to the nomadic Somalilander.

2. Global Responses

With the interconnectedness of global concerns becoming increasingly clear and more widely accepted, international migration and its myriad implications, including remittance flows, have gradually gained prominence on the international agenda.[12] The international community is seeking solutions to the challenges posed by 21st century migration as well as methods to harness the opportunities presented by this phenomenon. "Recent years have witnessed a growing appreciation of the need to maximize the contribution that migrants make to poverty reduction and sustainable development in their countries of origin."[13] With this increased appreciation of the potential of remittances as a development tool, remittance-sending countries are beginning to implement policies more conducive to the free and secure flow of these funds; "remittances are attracting growing attention from policy makers at the highest levels in both developed and developing countries."[14]

The United Nations (UN) reacted to remittances at the International Conference on Financing for Development in Monterrey, Mexico in 2002 by highlighting the importance of reducing the transfer costs of remittances in order to "create opportunities for development-oriented investments."[15] In 2003, with Resolution 58/208, the UN also noted the importance of remittances while "stressing the need to consider the various dimensions of this issue in a sustainable development perspective." In the same document, a high-level dialogue on migration and development was scheduled for the 2006 UN General Assembly (GA).[16] In an August 2005 report, the Secretary-General suggested that "actions to improve the impact of remittances on development" be a round table discussion topic at the 2006 GA.[17]

The African continent, especially south of the Sahara, has extremely limited formal banking structures; not surprisingly, the region also has a high rate of *hawala* users. Subsistence living in much of Africa is endemic and the success of poverty alleviation programs has been minimal. The African Union and the New Partnership for Africa's Development (NEPAD) both call on the African diaspora to contribute to the mobilization of the financial resources necessary for the successful development of the continent, but neither organization mentions "remittances" outright in their strategic plans of 2003 and 2001, respectively.

Overall global responses are high but there is a need for leadership in some southern African countries to become more active on the matter. However, today's focus on development contrasted with the concurrent silence regarding the human security threat of transfers being frozen is worrisome.

3. The Dilemma

As a result of its minimal regulation and vulnerability to misuse, *hawala* is seen by some as a threat to international security, "a financial tool of terrorism,"[18] and has therefore been targeted as such with crippling ramifications, especially in the wake of 9/11. However, awareness of the humanitarian component of this issue is growing; even recent news articles refer to migrants and the recipients of their remittances as a "non-combatant casualty of the war on terror," who are now faced with cumbersome new transfer regulations in the current security context.[19]

The *9/11 Commission Report* states that the "investigation has uncovered no evidence that the 9/11 conspirators employed *hawala*,"[20] however Al-Qaida's use of the system to move money at other times is well documented. "Bin Laden relied on the established *hawala* networks operating in Pakistan, in Dubai, and throughout the Middle East to transfer funds efficiently." The organization "frequently moved the money it raised by *hawala*. In some ways, Al-Qaeda had no choice…the banking system [in Afghanistan] was antiquated and undependable formal banking was risky due to the scrutiny that Al-Qaeda received after the August 1998 East Africa embassy bombings."[21] Following the attacks in New York, the United States government shut down the *hawala* channel presumed to be transferring funds for Al-Qaida. An unintended consequence of this act was the swift and devastating effect this halt in remittances had on the people of Somalia; stopping *hawala transfers to this country was* "tantamount to condemning hundreds of thousand of Somalis to a slow death."[22] Their remittance channel, their lifeline, was cut.

There is a dichotomy in the security implications presented by the *hawala* system. On one hand, limited regulation makes the system susceptible to misuse by individuals or organizations seeking to veil their economic activity, and therefore the system should be shut down. On the other hand, the *hawala* system, which operates in parts of the world where banking structures are non-existent, offers a method for migrants to provide their families in their home countries with the funds necessary for life's essentials, and therefore the system should be safeguarded at all costs.

4. Implications

Remittances are a very effective tool that individual migrants can use to contribute to the survival of their families and the betterment of their homelands. The disparity between the populations in developing and developed nations continues to challenge our world. The global community has the responsibility to facilitate these acts of giving back, of remitting, and in this act to contribute to the empowerment of the populations who are indeed helping themselves. The security of remittance flows is the question that must be addressed – but security in this case must be defined in all its facets: the recipient, the sender, individual states, regions, and the international community as a whole.

The presence of remittances on the international agenda is a positive sign, but the focus on their development potential is disconcerting. What protections are being put in place to preserve access to the resources made possible by the remittances to poor families, which are subsistence tools? How will policy discussions safeguard this very distinct body of remittances? The general absence in policy discourse of the human security threat posed by the blockage of remittance flows demonstrates that the subject is not being addressed in its entirety. Media and research mention the catastrophic consequences of paralyzed remittance systems, a reiteration of their value as a lifeline, however, the policy dialectic more often heard is limited to "remittances as a development tool."

Although subsistence and development are indeed linked, the two are perhaps more successfully addressed in parallel, and so should they be with regards to remittances. As a general rule, targeting only development is not a sufficient response to the immediacy of subsistence living needs. Such is the case for the group most at risk, which is the population highly dependent on remittances received through *hawala* for the majority of their household income.

5. Future Scenarios

Remittances have the potential to affect the following either positively or negatively; some issues could be affected more directly than others, some more immediately than others. The outcome depends on how the international community reflects the topic in policy but also on how broadly and creatively we choose to think.

- Access to food and water
- Access to medical care
- Access to education
- Human security

- Diversification of household incomes
- Poverty alleviation and poverty reduction
- Unemployment and underemployment
- Investment and/or savings opportunities

- Entrepreneurship
- Strengthening of economies

- Good governance
- Civil society
- Political participation of expatriates
- Circular migration

- Empowerment of individuals
- Sense of ownership and pride
- Expanding opportunities and experiences

There is no shortage of recommendations on how to better the context in which people who currently depend upon remittance flows currently find themselves, especially in terms of economic policy: issues that require further examination include lowering transfer fees, incorporating the informal sector into the formal, establishing programs that encourage investment of remittances, combining remittance policies with macro-economic policies, facilitating banking services, and developing more efficient data collection systems. Studies by the World Bank, the International Monetary Fund, the Global Commission on Migration, as well as various independent and UN reports have all been prolific with ideas for facilitating the free flow of remittances. For the September 2006 General Assembly meeting on migration, a *Compendium of Recommendations on International Migration and Development*[23] has been drafted by the UN, gathering in one document a treasure trove of thought, with no less than eight recommendations pertaining to remittances, although most recommendations come with specific reference to development.

If the path towards increasing the security of remittance flows is through the maximum use of the funds as a development tool, so be it. However, policy makers must be made aware of the degree of vulnerability of a portion of the recipients, an issue which must draw attention. Even one human life at risk is a sufficiently compelling reason to reflect and act.

6. Policy Recommendations

The following recommendations (meant to complement the widely-known recommendations on remittances as a development tool) refer to the informal *hawala* system specifically and target – for protection – the low-income population most vulnerable to suffer should remittance flows be halted.

Remittances used for subsistence living must be considered separately from remittances used as a development tool.
Remittances should be considered in their context and in their application. The term "remittance" is used as a overarching label for money transfers by migrants to their families in their countries of origin. However, remittances are defined by many factors, including how they are used. It is inappropriate to treat funds used for survival in the same manner as funds directed at investment.

Policy should reflect an awareness of the diversity of the uses of remittance flows and their various implications. Special attention, protection, must be given to the cases where remittance flows represent the "oxygen" or lifeline of the recipients.

In parallel to their roundtable discussion on improving the development impact of remittances, the upcoming General Assembly should also discuss "subsistence remittances." Policy specific to safeguarding "subsistence remittances" should be drafted.

The recipients of "subsistence remittances" should be identified.
Identifying the population whose human security is most threatened by the blockage of remittances is essential for improving the protection of these individuals, as well as the free flow of their remittances.

One method for identifying the population in question is to improve the currently sporadic data collection on how recipients spend their remittances, and how much remittances represent of household incomes. This should be done with the specific aim of identifying those most reliant on remittances for survival. Employing the brokers on the receiving end to facilitate a survey upon dispersal of funds would be a key source of information that could be used to pinpoint the most vulnerable individuals.

Special attention should be drawn to highly vulnerable subsistence remittance-recipient regions.

Regions that lack formal, efficient, and reliable banking and money transfer structures present a special challenge. These regions include not only much of sub-Saharan Africa and failed states, but many overwhelmingly impoverished areas, notably refugee camps. In these regions, the informal transfer system is more commonly used and creates the most extensive data gaps on remittances.

In considering "subsistence remittances," particular attention should be given to these geographic areas. Relevant international organizations, regional organizations, and state structures should collaborate on the study of "subsistence remittances" in these regions.

The hawala system should be better documented.

The value of transfers passed through the *hawala* system is presently thought to be underestimated by 50 percent or more. Improving the documentation of the system and its users is essential to making it more secure. Developing alternatives or encouraging the use of existing ones is not the only option. The overall improvement of the *hawala* system should also be undertaken, especially as *hawala* users prefer and trust this transfer method (for reasons explained earlier in this brief) and are unlikely to discard it easily.

It is this very same population, the regular users of *hawala* and the hawala system's brokers, who are most knowledgeable about the system; they should be involved in the development of better data collection on the volume of transfers, the source of the funds, their application, and the identity of senders and recipients.

Hawala users should be engaged in preventing the misuse of the hawala system.

The brokers and regular users of the *hawala* system are in a position to identify how the system might be misused for terrorist financing, money laundering, and other criminal purposes. Their efforts would have the concurrent benefit of improving their own security as well as that of the international community.

Governments and policy makers should partner with *hawala* brokers in anti-terrorism/criminal efforts.

References

[1] *Global Economic Prospects: Economic Implications of Remittances and Migration*, The World Bank, 2006, p. 85, available at http://www.earthinstitute.columbia.edu/cgsd/remittances/documents/Ratha.2006.pdf#search='Global%20Economic%20Prospects%3A%20Economic%20Implications%20of%20Remittances%20and%20Migration%E2%80%9D'.
[2] *Ibid.*, p. 87.
[3] *Ibid.*, p. xi.
[4] *Migration in an Interconnected World: New Directions for Action*, The Global Commission on International Migration, October 2005, pp. 1 and 7, available at http://www.gcim.org/attachements/gcim-complete-report-2005.pdf.
[5] *Resource Flows to Africa: An Update on Statistical Trends*, United Nations Office of the Special Adviser on Africa, 2005.
[6] The World Bank, *op. cit.,* note 1, p. 121.
[7] United Nations Office of the Special Adviser on Africa, *op. cit.,* note 5.
[8] "Disaster Beckons as U.S. Cuts Lifeline," UN Office for the Coordination of Humanitarian Affairs, IRINnews.org, 8 November 2001.
[9] R. Kent, K. von Hippel, with M. Bradbury, *Social Facilitation, Development and the Diaspora*, The International Policy Institute, King's College London, November 2004, p. 9.
[10] The World Bank, *op. cit.,* note 1, pp. 135-137.
[11] "Two-hour remittance service," *Middle East Personal Finance News Wire*, March 23, 2006.
[12] *Compendium of Recommendations on International Migration and Development*, United Nations Department of Economic and Social Affairs, 2006, p. 3 "...most of the major United Nations conferences held in the 1990s addressed relevant aspects of the issue and consequently have set collectively the elements of a potential United Nations framework for addressing the issues and concerns raised by international migration, particularly as it relates to development." Available at http://www.un.org/esa/population/publications/UN_GCIM/UN_GCIM_ITTMIG.Pdf.
[13] The Global Commission on International Migration, *op. cit.,* note 4, p. 8.
[14] The World Bank, *op. cit.,* note 1, pp. 85 and 96.
[15] "Report of the International Conference on Financing for Development," United Nations Document A/CONF.198/11, Monterrey, Mexico, March 18-22, 2002, p. 5, §18, available at http://www.un.org/esa/ffd/aconf198-11.pdf.
[16] *International Migration and Development*, General Assembly Resolution A/RES/58/208, February 13, 2004, p. 3, available at http://www.un.org/esa/population/publications/fourthcoord2005/A_RES_58_208.pdf.
[17] *Globalization and Interdependence: International Migration and Development*, Report of the Secretary-General, General Assembly Document A/60/205, August 8, 2005, p. 7, §28, available at http://daccessdds.un.org/doc/UNDOC/GEN/N05/455/19/PDF/N0545519.pdf?OpenElement.
[18] N. Passas, "Hawala and other informal value transfer systems: how to regulate them?," US International Information Programs, 2003, available at http://usinfo.state.gov.
[19] P. Bowring, "The War on Third-World Remittances," *International Herald Tribune*, November 28, 2005.
[20] *The 9/11 Commission Report*, The National Commission on Terrorist Attacks Upon the United States, July 22, 2004, p. 499, available at http://www.gpoaccess.gov/911/pdf/fullreport.pdf.
[21] *Ibid.*, p.171.
[22] UN Office for the Coordination of Humanitarian Affairs, *op. cit.,* note 8; United Nations Department of Economic and Social Affairs, *op. cit.,* note 12.

CHAPTER 17

EDITORIAL OF POLICY BRIEF ON INFORMAL REMITTANCE FLOWS AND THEIR IMPLICATIONS FOR GLOBAL SECURITY

NAYEF R.F. AL-RODHAN

Dr. Nayef R.F. Al-Rodhan is Senior Scholar in Geostrategy and Director of the Program on the Geopolitical Implications of Globalization and Transnational Security at the Geneva Centre for Security Policy, Geneva, Switzerland

1. Review and Critique

Remittance flows are a vital source of income for individuals within various countries around the world.[1] In 2005, an astounding estimated $232 billion in remittances were sent globally, an increase from $68.6 billion in 1990.[2] Dependence on this system has become an issue of international security, particularly in the aftermath of the events of September 11, 2001. Due to the misuse of this system by terrorist organizations and other potentially harmful actors, the international community has, over the past few years, demanded reform of the system in order to better regulate it. However, in so doing, some of the most beneficial aspects of the informal network may be at stake and therefore prevent many people in certain regions of the world from receiving the only income to which they have access.

As indicated in the *Global Economic Prospects 2006* report produced by the World Bank, "governments in destination and origin countries can sharpen the developmental impact of remittances through the application of appropriate policies."[3] Both have a large role to play in monitoring and improving the way that remittances can be tracked without disrupting the flow of this vital lifeline. For instance, currently the cost of remittances could be greatly impacted by a system that protects the percentage charged to even the smallest transfers.[4]

The largest dilemma for states is that confidentiality and a non-governmental, non-institutional system of money transfer are exactly what make the informal transfer of remittances so attractive for many migrants and their families. It is these very qualities – confidentiality, lack of paper trails, and institutional accountability – that make such remittances a concern for governments. Often based in countries where there is an existing lack of trust in more formal banking systems or there is no access to formal banking, the informal transfer, or *hawala* system, has grown over the years. Specifically, *hawala* is an informal banking system in which funds are transferred internationally, without being physically moved. The main users of the system reside in the developed world and transfer funds to recipients in the developing world. The system makes monitoring the flow of remittances extremely difficult for states and therefore attractive not only for those who do not trust formal, traditional banking channels but also for those who would like to transfer funds illegally and undetected. This is what prompted the United States (US) to close banking institutions in Somalia in November, 2001 as it was believed that certain institutions (Al-Barakat, the Somali *hawala* group, in this case) were used to deliver funds to Al-Qaida and Osama Bin Laden, an accusation that was denied by the group's founder and chairman.[5]

Miriam Fugfugosh[6] outlines these issues very well in her policy brief and indicates where the most pressing problems lie, both for the states where immigrants currently reside as well as for the state where their families have remained. Additionally, she clearly identifies where the policy challenges are for states, which must find quick solutions for dealing with these informal networks that are so often used by mass groups of people. How do you build trust in a formal system in countries where a history of corruption within governmental entities has led the population to – rationally – mistrust the state's formal institutions? How can you bring these same people to trust that the remittances upon which they depend for survival will be safely and securely transferred at the state level?

2. Dilemmas and Our Recommendations

The solutions required to solve some of these problems may at first seem obvious. However, the root causes and solutions are not so easily defined. The humanitarian need for remittances remains critical to most of those receiving funds in this manner; if states such as the US choose to cut this lifeline, larger humanitarian problems will become a reality. How these flows can be used as a means for reducing poverty should also be at the forefront of state thinking.

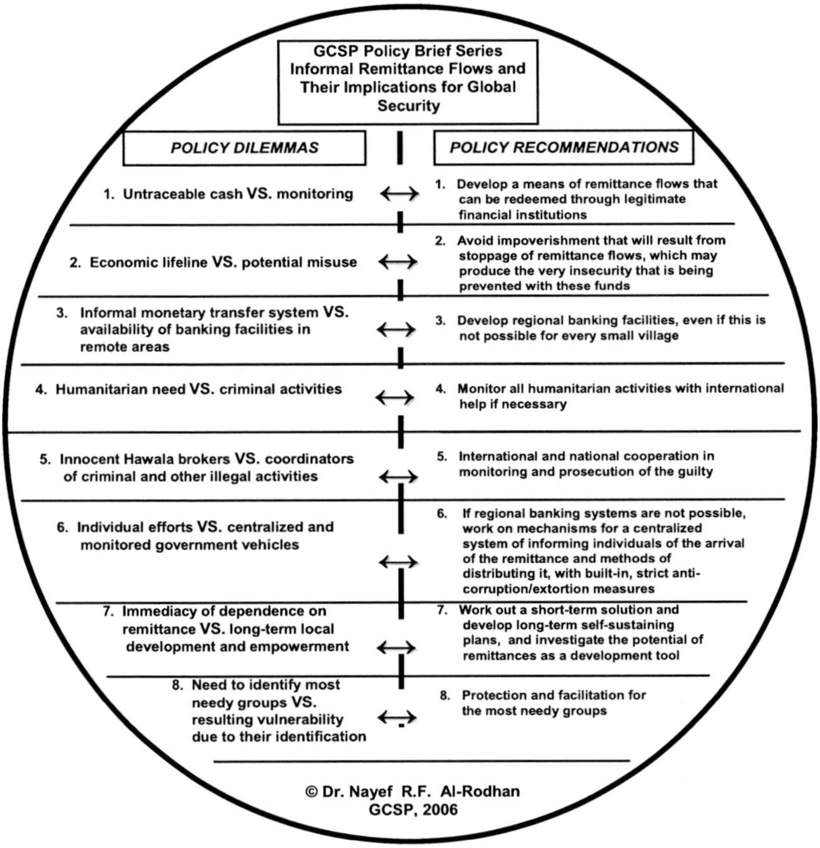

Informal remittance flows are not only a large source of insecurity for some governments, however, as mentioned, they also serve as the very lifeblood for many individuals. Thus, doing away with them totally would render large groups of people incapable of taking care of themselves. How do governments reconcile the aspects of remittances that contribute to global insecurity while still allowing for the free flow of funds that are necessary for sustainability and economic development?

The large dilemmas for states rest in the inability to monitor remittances. Cash flows may be easier to trace, but remittances leave virtually no paper trail in some cases. States should work with those that distribute as well as those that give and receive remittances in order to develop means so that these funds could be channeled through legitimate financial institutions. This would also reduce potential misuse and therefore would avoid the potential poverty that may result from halting remittances flows. This potential disruption (as was the case in 2001 when the US closed Al-Barakat[7]) would have devastating effects in the country to which the remittances are sent.

The humanitarian need for securing the flow of remittances must be carefully balanced with the need to prevent the widespread misuse of this system for criminal activities. This requires that the international community work together with governments, clans, and banks in order to develop effective monitoring solutions. This is also the case when an innocent (in some cases) *hawala* broker is simply trying to do his job but his efforts are undermined by those brokers who are coordinating criminal activities through their post. This leads to further sources of insecurity within these communities beyond the obvious far-reaching effects of transnational terrorism. International institutions, national institutions, and governments must work to monitor and identify those who are innocent and work within the legal framework of the system. Governments have a responsibility to protect these individuals – and their funds – from harm. Simultaneously, efforts need to be coordinated in the identification and prosecution of those that are utilizing the system for criminal activities.

All of these recommendations address the short-term effects of remittance flows and their impact in dealing with security. Nevertheless, it is also important to also think about how to best shape the remittance system in the future, regardless of the reforms required. Poor populations' dependence on remittances is clear; however, the international community should also work towards long-term local development and empowerment in the countries where remittances are being sent. For example, micro-loans to women have been phenomenally successful in some instances.[8] While this seems like a large order for the international community, small changes are happening sporadically in Africa and other parts of the world, but larger international players such as the European Union and the US need to work out these short-term solutions. The focus should then also be on what can be done in order to implement long-term, self-sustaining plans to reduce the dependence of these communities on remittances.

3. Conclusion

The number of communities that are dependent on these funds is staggering. Formal systems of transfer and banking have, for a number of reasons, co-existed with these informal networks. Trust has been built within this traditional system due to its informal networks and its reliability in countries such as Somalia, where there are no formal networks available for individual use. With the advent of new technologies that can provide new opportunities for solving some of these dilemmas, states need to find solutions that not only provide security in the system for those wishing to transfer funds but also allow for policing functions, when necessary, by the states involved. Only then will the remittance system help produce long-term stability and security for individuals as well as for states and thus the entire international system.

References

[1] In the "Global Economic Prospects 2006" report produced by the World Bank, remittances were specifically addressed. The report stated that "in aggregate, remittances are more than twice as [sic] the size of international aid flows," p. xi. The report may be downloaded in its entirety at http://web.worldbank.org/external/default/main?contentMDK=20709766&menuPK=615470&theSitePK=612501&pagePK=64218950&piPK=64218883.

[2] *Ibid.*, p. 88.

[3] *Ibid.*, p. xv.

[4] *Ibid.*, p. xv.

[5] "Disaster Beckons as U.S. Cuts Lifeline," *UN Office for the Coordination of Humanitarian Affairs*, IRINnews.org, November 8, 2001.

[6] The policy brief may be viewed in its entirety in Chapter 16.

[7] For an entire overview of the US decision to close Al-Barakat, please see http://news.bbc.co.uk/2/hi/in_depth/world/2002/september_11_one_year_on/2219680.stm. Al-Barakat was an informal firm that handled a large amount of remittance transfers for numerous countries at the time of its closure because of alleged links to Al-Qaida. The disruption in remittance flows had devastating effects for the country of Somalia, a state lacking in formal banking systems.

[8] See, for example, "Empowering Women," *BBC News Online*, October 6, 2000, accessed at http://news.bbc.co.uk/2/hi/africa/960206.stm.

CHAPTER 18

PEACE OPERATIONS: REFLECTIONS OF, RESPONSES TO, AND VICTIMS OF, GLOBALIZATION

THIERRY TARDY

Dr. Thierry Tardy is Course Director of the European Training Course in Security Policy at the Geneva Centre for Security Policy, Geneva, Switzerland

Abstract
A peace operation is an activity through which states deploy military and civilian resources – via an international organization or not – to handle a given crisis in a third state. Peace operations are about international security, policy responses to conflicts and to failing states, and military interventions, as well as about human security, good governance, and liberal peace. Each of these different areas is influenced by the globalization process insofar as globalization shapes the nature of conflicts and the overall framework of their management (actors, policies, underlying principles).

By addressing the different challenges and responses that peace operations are facing, this paper argues that peace operations are simultaneously a product of globalization, a response to globalization, and a victim of globalization.

1. Policy Challenges

(a) Peace Operations as a Reflection of Globalization

The policy challenges that peace operations are confronted with in a globalized world can be put into two categories. At the macro level, globalization accentuates the disconnect between, on the one hand, the general approach to conflict resolution through peace operations, which is still largely dominated by a state-centric, Westphalian conception of international relations, and, on the other hand, the nature of conflicts and of the actors that play a role in their management, which refers less and less to a purely state-centric approach.[1] Second, peace operations suffer from the disconnect between the needs of recipient states, on the one hand, and what the intervening actors – be they states or international organizations – are ready to offer, in terms of human, military, financial capabilities, and political support, on the other. It follows that peace operations are often more responses to the concerns of intervening states than responses to the needs of a given conflict. Third, one characteristic of globalization is the erosion of state sovereignty, and while peace operations are partly aimed at restoring that lost sovereignty, paradoxically they also play on this erosion through their intrusive nature.

At the micro level, policy challenges concern the ability of international organizations – the United Nations (UN) and regional organizations – to understand the complexity of the conflicts they are dealing with, as well as to plan and run complex operations (which raises the issue of their reform). Challenges also include the extent to which peace operations benefit from a strategic vision, the coordination of the multitude of actors involved, the respect of legal and moral principles by peacekeepers, and local ownership of the whole process.[2] All these elements are not necessarily directly influenced by globalization, yet the complexity of current peace operations, which by and large gives birth to the above-mentioned policy challenges, is a reflection of globalization. By extension, peace operations are a reflection of globalization in the sense that they reflect the interdependence of processes and actors that characterize globalization.

2. Responses to Policy Challenges

(a) Peace Operations as a Response to Globalization

In many ways, peace operations can be seen as a response to the negative effects of globalization. They are aimed at providing some sort of stability and regulation in places that are characterized by a high degree of instability and deregulation (failed states), which are largely by-products of globalization. In many cases, they are also aimed at reconstructing a state, which is seen as the central element of the international system, and possibly as a protection against the negative effects of globalization. From a Northern perspective, peace operations may also be answers to globalization insofar as they should prevent the spillover of security concerns from the South to the North.

In this context, responses to the identified policy challenges vary from one peace-operations actor to another, but the following trends can be identified.

The first trend is the widening of the range of activities handled by peace operations and that are directly linked with, though not created by, the globalization process (examples are refugee flows, organized crime, or the arrest of war criminals).

Second, in response to the mistakes of the early 1990s in the Balkans and in order to better reflect both the complexity of conflicts and the constraints of the intervening actors, one can see a certain form of "rationalization" of peace operations. In the UN context, this led to the reform process initiated by the *Brahimi Report*,[3] which advocates that the UN do less but do it better. In general terms and for all categories of actors, peace operations should respond to clear mandates backed by credible means and should not embark on impossible missions. This leads to a general reluctance to be involved in any form of peace enforcement, or even to be engaged in the protection of civilians, for fear of the related costs and risks of mission creep.

A division of labor between different peace-operation actors is also promoted, based on comparative advantages and/or regional expertise. One consequence of globalization has been the emergence of regional actors that are supposed to share the security burden with international actors, the UN in particular.[4] Regionalization of peace operations is one dimension, with organizations such as the North Atlantic Treaty Organisation (NATO), the European Union (EU), the African Union, or the Organization for Security and Co-operation in Europe (OSCE) playing an increasing role. Simultaneously, these institutions have developed know-how in peace operations that, in turn, has created a theoretical division of labor (NATO is in charge of the military aspects; the EU, of the civilian and economic aspects; the OSCE, of elections and institution-building, etc.). This evolution and the necessary coordination of these actors have led to a wide range of initiatives to enhance relations among international organizations both at the headquarters level and in the field (especially the case between the UN and the EU, and to a lesser extent between the UN and NATO and the African Union).

3. Dilemmas

In the context of the rationalization of peace operations, some important political and moral dilemmas persist that impact on the coherence of peace operations. One dimension of globalization is the increased flow of information: this impacts on both the level of awareness of conscience-shocking situations and on the degree of scrutiny that peace operations have to undergo.

Subsequently, one dilemma comes from the necessity for states to somehow respond to conscience-shocking situations while taking account of the political and legal constraints that are attached to any kind of intervention in a third state. Such a dilemma is apparent in the case of Darfur and around the implementation of the concept of "responsibility to protect."[5]

A second important dilemma that almost all peace operations face stems from the very objective of the operations. Through the deployment of a peace operation, especially in a peacebuilding mode, intervening states impose a political model ("liberal peace"),[6] without having analyzed the political and moral implications for the recipient state.

Third, all peace operations that have a humanitarian dimension have illustrated the dilemma contained in the link between humanitarian activity and politics. Questions that follow are about the politicization of humanitarian aid and the consequences for its impartiality, but also the efficacy of humanitarian aid when it is completely separate from the state actors present on the ground.[7]

Finally, a persisting dilemma stems from the difficulty to square the concept of military intervention – which, after all is what a peace operation is about – with the reluctance of intervening states to take risks – and to resort to force – in the implementation of their mandate.[8] In most cases, while operations fall within Chapter VII of the UN Charter and mandates include the protection of civilians, force protection takes precedence over the protection of locals, regardless of what the mandate of the operation says, and contributing states tend to opt for a minimalist understanding of their mandates.

4. Implications

(a) Peace Operations as a Victim of Globalization

Combined with the policy challenges, the above-mentioned dilemmas tend to have negative implications on peace operations, which leads to the argument that peace operations are in a way a victim of globalization.

First and foremost, peace operations are half-hearted measures that are always imperfect responses to complex situations. As they fail to fully grasp the evolutions imposed by globalization and reflect state hesitation *vis-à-vis* the deployment of armed force, peace operations are condemned to be the lowest common denominator of state action and miss the real needs of a conflict zone. Even worse, state indecisiveness may materialize when peace operations are launched in lieu of a more decisive operation aimed at tackling a given conflict in earnest. Such was the case with the UN operation in Bosnia and Herzegovina between 1992 and 1995, and more recently with the African Union operation in Darfur, where peace operations reflect a certain willingness to do something as much as they reveal an absence of commitment.

In the same vein, peace operations may appear as the main axis of the response by the "international community" to a particular conflict when they should be just one component of the response. Most peace operations tend to deal with the consequences of a conflict, while overlooking the causes and politics behind it. In the Democratic Republic of the Congo or in Darfur, peace operations seem to attract most of the attention at the expense of conflict resolution. It follows that many of the activities conducted by peace operations (in the field of DDR,[9] for example) are likely to produce no tangible effect as long as the conflict is not addressed at its roots.

Finally, peace operations lack strategic vision, as such a vision appears to contradict the political, moral, and military constraints associated with the operations. In other words, the primary need for a strategic vision cannot be met as long as peace operations are supposed to tackle highly complex situations with ambiguous mandates that are inadequately backed.

Peace operations are victims of globalization because they suffer from the loss of bearings that globalization implies.

5. Future Trajectories/Scenarios

The future evolution of peace operations depends on various underlying factors that have to do with local perceptions of peace operations, state practices, the evolution of international organizations and their ability to reform, and the evolution of norms regulating interventions.

To confine our analysis to three elements, the future of peace operations will be shaped by their legitimacy, their efficacy, and their accountability. The legitimacy of peace operations is to be found at the three levels of the legitimacy of the body issuing the mandate (UN Security Council, Council of the EU, OSCE, other), of the degree of acceptance of the operation by locals (and subsequently its level of intrusiveness), and of the policies implemented within peace operations, including the behavior of peacekeepers.

Second, the efficacy of operations will remain an element of concern, especially in the field of rapid deployment, as will the quality of the personnel being deployed and their ability to conduct "robust peacekeeping."[10] In the case of the UN, the propensity of Western states to support operations will remain of key importance.

Third, peace operations of the future will have to be more accountable for what they do and what their personnel do within their framework. This accountability issue can be seen as one positive evolution associated with globalization and the publicity of operations.

In this context, the division of tasks among the various actors in peace operations will be one of utmost importance.[11] Burden sharing between the UN and regional organizations is at stake here, as is the possible role that non-state actors (non-governmental organizations, as well as private security companies and other private actors) will play in future peace operations. As for the role of regional organizations, a lot will depend on the propensity of the EU and NATO to assume more of the burden, as much as on the ability of other regional organizations, the African Union in particular, to equip themselves so as to become full-fledged actors in peace operations. In the short term, based on the situation in Darfur, it is unlikely that the African Union will be able to take over much of what the UN is currently doing in Africa. As for the role played by the EU and NATO, one risk is the accentuation of an existing tendency: two-speed crisis management,[12] i.e., a strong dichotomy between crisis management implemented by wealthy and politically strong institutions such as the EU and NATO, and the crisis management of the poor, mainly conducted by countries of the South, though largely financed by the North. By extension, one could see a division between some peace-operations actors (Western states, NATO, EU) that fully benefit from globalization in the conduct of their peace operations (in terms of military equipment, communications, and logistics) and others (developing states, UN, African Union) that have not yet reached that level of modernity.

6. Policy Recommendations

Policy recommendations must be seen as ways to ensure that peace operations are better able to benefit more from the positive effect of globalization while minimizing its negative effects. The following 10 recommendations draw on existing ones and look at peace operations beyond the UN framework:

1. Mandates of peace operations must be clear and achievable;
2. Strategic vision must guide each peace operation;
3. Division of labor between the UN and regional organizations must be clarified at the legal, political, and operational levels;
4. All actors in peace operations must be better coordinated, and an integrated approach must be sought whenever possible;
5. The peacekeeping doctrines of each organization must be clarified and harmonized;
6. Standards of peacekeeping must be developed;
7. Regional organizations must act in accordance with the UN Charter;
8. Mechanisms must be developed to guarantee the accountability of missions and of peacekeepers;
9. Good-quality leadership of operations is a *sine qua non*; and

10. Peace operations must be run in full coordination with local populations.

References

[1] See M. Kaldor, *New and Old Wars. Organized Violence in a Global Era* (Cambridge: Polity Press, 1999).
[2] See T. Tardy, "The Brahimi Report: Four Years On," Proceedings of the Annual GCSP Peace Operations Workshop, No. 3, Geneva, June 2004, and "Pursuing Security in the Post-Conflict Phase: Implications for Current and Future Peace Operations," (co-authored with R. Mani), Report on the Annual GCSP Peace Operations Workshop, No. 4, Geneva, November 2005.
[3] For the UN, see "Report of the Panel on United Nations Peace Operations" ("Brahimi Report"), United Nations, A/55/305, August 21, 2000. Also see "Peace Operations 2010," Department of Peacekeeping Operations, United Nations, November 2005.
[4] See M. Pugh and W.P. Singh Sidhu (eds.), *The United Nations and Regional Security: Europe and Beyond* (Boulder, CO: Lynne Rienner, 2003).
[5] See P. Williams and A. Bellamy, "The Responsibility to Protect and the Crisis in Darfur," *Security Dialogue*, Vol. 36, No. 1, March 2005.
[6] See D. Chandler, "Imposing the Liberal Peace?," *International Peacekeeping*, Vol. 11, No. 1, Spring 2004.
[7] See N. MacFarlane, *Politics and Humanitarian Action*, Occasional Paper No. 41, The Thomas Watson Institute for International Studies, 2000.
[8] See S. Chesterman, *The Use of Force in UN Peace Operations*, External Study, UN Peacekeeping Best Practices Unit, United Nations, August 2004; and I. Johnstone, "Dilemmas of Robust Peace Operations," in *Annual Review of Global Peace Operations 2006*, Center on International Cooperation (London: Lynne Rienner, 2006).
[9] DDR: Demobilization, Disarmament and Reintegration of former combatants.
[10] Johnstone, *op. cit.*, note 8.
[11] See Folke Bernadotte Academy, "Meeting the Challenges of Peace Operations: Cooperation and Coordination," Challenges Project – Phase II Concluding Report, 2003-2006.
[12] See R. Thakur and D. Malone, "Tribes within the UN," *The Hindustan Times*, November 20, 2000.

CHAPTER 19

EDITORIAL OF POLICY BRIEF ON PEACE OPERATIONS: REFLECTIONS OF, RESPONSES TO, AND VICTIMS OF, GLOBALIZATION

NAYEF R.F. AL-RODHAN

Dr. Nayef R.F. Al-Rodhan is Senior Scholar in Geostrategy and Director of the Program on the Geopolitical Implications of Globalization and Transnational Security at the Geneva Centre for Security Policy, Geneva, Switzerland

1. Review and Critique

A peace operation, whether mandated through the United Nations (UN) or as a unilateral move by a state, is a politically, economically, and militarily complicated task. The question of state sovereignty is a key element in the successful implementation of peace operations and in their lasting impact in post-conflict situations. Since the first deployment of troops in a peace operation in 1956 to assist in the Suez crisis, these operations have been facing obstacles on both operational and political levels. Naturally, such management tools in post-conflict and crisis situations have been duly affected by globalization.

In the history of the UN alone, there have been more than 60 peace operations since 1948.[1] These have made a large contribution to the security and stability of the international system when they have been effectively deployed. As one might imagine, there is significant debate within the international community regarding operations and their effectiveness. These missions have been viewed and implemented very differently and are even referred to by different names depending on the geographic location of the mandate, the country sending troops, and the political necessity surrounding a specific operation.[2] Peace operations are by nature a transnational solution for inter- and intra-state conflicts.

Thierry Tardy, in his policy brief "Peace Operations: Reflections of, Responses to, and Victims of, Globalization,"[3] addresses this issue. He contends that "peace operations are simultaneously a product of globalization, a response to globalization, and a victim of globalization." He claims that, due to the fact that globalization shapes and impacts the way in which conflicts develop and the overall framework of their management, the impact is largely felt throughout the peace-operations community and it is an important aspect to assess.

2. Dilemmas and Our Recommendations

While the dilemmas raised between states have been at the forefront of discussions related to peace operations in recent years due to the conflicts in Darfur and Côte d'Ivoire (among others), peace operations have received further attention. Presented on the following page are eight dilemmas and our recommended state action for dealing with these issues.

When discussing UN peace operations with states in terms of proper actions and reactions in conflict situations, many dilemmas and solutions are raised. However, the dilemmas that we have identified here provide some of the most fundamental challenges that states face: namely, the need for a clear UN mandate, as well as diplomatic solutions versus the need for peace operations. In addition, the responsibility to intervene quickly to prevent humanitarian disasters and the logistical ability of states to get involved place large burdens on a state's ability to react and respond. The recommendations in this section provide potential means of improvement. All operations need to be led by a UN mandate wherever possible; diplomatic efforts need to be extensive, multilateral, and coordinated with early conflict detection and clear post-conflict plans.

Furthermore, state sovereignty is a large stumbling block for most nation-states. Related is the dilemma between true humanitarian peace operations and those that have ulterior political, financial and/or security motives. The only effective way to deal with such issues is to guarantee the transparency, credibility, accountability, and non-financial remuneration of missions and to empower individuals in

conflict-torn areas. It is also important to facilitate shared responsibility and empowerment of the conflict areas and in the regional organizations to ensure a timely withdrawal of troops to avoid perceptions of neo-colonialism.

Finally, the type of personnel that make up peacekeeping forces and the way in which they conduct themselves are critical to the success of missions. Respect for local customs, in terms of dress codes and etiquette, versus the potentially problematic behavior of peacekeeping forces must be kept in proper balance. Only then will states be able to conduct such missions effectively. The best way of ensuring this is to educate peacekeepers about these cultural sensitivities, as well as to include personnel that have ethnic and religious relevance to the area of conflict. There must also be strict, accountable and ethical behavior by peacekeepers. In this way, these dilemmas can be dealt with in a meaningful way that does not prevent the success of such operations.

3. Conclusion

The impact that the globalization process has had on peacekeeping operations is complex and can be seen at any given time from a number of angles. The dilemmas that we have presented here are very important to the success of such missions at both the state and regional levels. Without taking into consideration these eight dilemmas, states will not be able to properly deal with the challenges that they face when participating in UN mandates. By taking them into consideration and revising state responses in order to act in accordance with these recommendations, states will make conflict prevention and their reactions to conflicts much more successful and valuable in their contributions to transnational security.

References

[1] United Nations Peacekeeping Operations, http://www.un.org/Depts/dpko/dpko/bnote.htm.

[2] T. Tardy, "Introduction," in T. Tardy (ed.), *Peace Operations After 11 September 2001* (London and New York: Frank Cass, 2004), p. 2.

[3] For the brief in its entirety, please see Chapter 18.

CHAPTER 20

THE UNITED NATIONS AND THE CHALLENGES OF A GLOBALIZED WORLD: TOWARDS A QUANTUM LEAP FROM MULTILATERALISM TO GLOBALIZATION?

VICTOR-YVES GHEBALI

Dr. Victor-Yves Ghebali is Professor of Political Science at the Graduate Institute of International Studies, Geneva, Switzerland

Abstract
This paper offers an assessment of the main responses given by the United Nations (UN) to the challenges of globalization at the economic and collective security level, with the conclusion that those responses have been incomplete, if not paltry. Meant to address urgent challenges, the 2005 World Summit represented a missed opportunity because of a widespread nostalgia for old style sovereignty, as well as the dogmatic anti-UN stands of the present United States administration. Although a quantum leap from multilateralism to globalization is overdue, most of the UN member states are seemingly not ready to go beyond quick fixes.

1. Introduction

Like other concepts in the vocabulary of international relations, globalization has no accepted definition. However, the general understanding is that globalization entails a process of exponential increase of communications and transactions among and between state and non-state actors (at the interstate, transnational, and interpersonal level), accompanied by a relative decline in the traditional role of the state. It is also argued that globalization has opened a "post-Westphalian" era within what is becoming (according to Marshall McLuhan's prescient metaphor) a "global village." In a certain sense, globalization is not a new phenomenon. It has been underway for several decades, if not (according to some authors) centuries. Decisively accelerated by the revolution in information technologies, the concept of globalization acquired an even higher profile following the transition from bipolarity to multipolarity. After the dawning of the 21st century, globalization is a process in the making, whose long-term effects beyond the realm of economics are still unpredictable.

The development of globalization is affecting intergovernmental organizations. With the rare exception of the World Trade Organization (WTO), those organizations embody multilateralism – an inter-state driven process meant to regulate the conflictual and cooperative relationships of nation-states and, hence, *preserve* national sovereignties. By contrast, globalization restrains the capacity of nation-states to perform as fully sovereign entities in a world where there is still no true global governance. Because of its holistic mandate, the UN is at the heart of the conundrum. Over the last four decades, it managed to survive in a bipolar setting, in which the Charter's collective security system was simply unworkable. While the collapse of Communism abolished the iron law of bipolarity, the globalization process plunged the UN overnight into another existential crisis. At present, the UN has to rethink its approach, guiding principles, and operational tools to collective security, development, and human rights.

The UN acknowledged the necessity of meeting these challenges when it decided to hold, within the 2000 session of the General Assembly, a "Millennium Summit."[1] In a special preparatory report to the Summit, Secretary General Kofi Annan stated that the time had come for the UN to shift from multilateralism to globalization because "while the post-war multilateral system made it possible for the new globalization to emerge and flourish, globalization, in turn, has progressively rendered its designs antiquated."[2] Since then, the UN's major attempts to achieve such a quantum leap have been charted by the *Global Compact Initiative* (2000), the *Millennium Declaration* (2000), the *Millennium Development Goals* (2001), and the *World Summit Outcome Document* (2005) – as well as two special reports on UN reform, one from a High-level Panel on Threats, Challenges and Change (2004)[3] and another from the Secretary General himself (2005).[4] This paper analyzes the challenges that globalization poses to the UN as well as the responses given so far regarding development and collective security.

2. Policy Challenges, Responses, Dilemmas, and Implications: Development

(a) Policy Challenges

The continuous decline in official development aid, combined with the dramatic upsurge of economic globalization, convinced the UN that the state-centered and regulatory approach to development was leading to a dead end.

(b) Responses

As a consequence, the UN decided to establish a partnership with the private sector while also fixing a set of quantifiable goals to be achieved within the next 15 years. Launched by Kofi Annan in July 2000, the *Global Compact Initiative* aimed at encouraging transnational corporations to adhere to and respect (on a voluntary basis) ten fundamental norms concerning human rights, labor standards, protection of the environment, and anti-corruption measures. Given the longstanding hostility of the UN towards corporate business, the Initiative amounted to a dramatic politico-intellectual change. In parallel, the General Assembly adopted a roadmap, fixing eight "Millennium Development Goals" (MDGs) to be achieved by 2015 – halving extreme poverty and hunger, achieving universal primary education, empowering women and promoting gender equality, reducing under-five mortality by two thirds, reducing maternal mortality by three quarters, reversing the spread of diseases (especially HIV/AIDS and malaria), ensuring environmental sustainability, and creating a global partnership for development. Unsurprisingly, both initiatives became controversial.

(c) Dilemmas

Critics of the *Global Compact Initiative* labeled it a leonine deal, permitting transnational corporations to obtain a label of social respectability from the UN in exchange for token commitments. They challenged the very principle of a marriage between market goals and UN universal ideals and thus questioned Kofi Annan's assertion that a partnership with the private sector could simultaneously lead to sustainable development and responsible corporate business. Critics doubt that an agent basically driven by profit-making could really contribute to poverty reduction and are concerned that the privatization of the development process will create as many problems as it is supposed to solve – for instance, by providing (potential or actual) donor governments with a major excuse for evading responsibilities while compromising the UN's public image and ideals.[5]

The Millennium Development Goals have also been subject to different interpretations. While some experts praised their pragmatic approach, reconciling the economic and social objectives of development, others criticized them for focusing on quantitative (rather on qualitative) goals, as well as for offering no real added value. Actually, the MDGs are a re-clothing of previous goals that the 2005 World Summit Outcome Document has restated without additional obligations.[6]

(d) Implications

Admittedly, the problem of development needs to be solved with the involvement of non-state actors that play a central role in the process of economic globalization. However, even if the Global Compact Network represents a means to adapt the UN to the challenges of globalization, one cannot deny the risk that the goals of the Compact could only be achieved at an exorbitant price.

It must also be recognized that the MDGs have been formulated in an era when humanity has unprecedented resources to effectively solve most global problems – including hunger and extreme poverty. The trouble is that economic globalization as a force is undermining the social contract and that the most crucial development-related issues (trade, macroeconomic and adjustment policies, financial crises, etc.) are the preserve of other bodies outside the UN: the Bretton Woods institutions and the WTO. In the absence of appropriate empowerment to address such matters, the UN could hardly expect to be able to meet the relevant challenges of economic globalization. According to all odds, the achievement of the MDGs is less certain than ever.

3. Policy Challenges, Responses, Dilemmas, and Implications: Collective Security

(a) Policy Challenges

In sharp contrast with the case of development, a change in the UN's approach to collective security is needed not because of globalization, but as a direct consequence of the end of the Cold War. Indeed, the elimination of the risk of a global nuclear Armageddon gave way to a host of smaller-scale, interconnected, and less predictable threats of a basically non-military, transnational, and intra-state nature: terrorism, organized criminality, aggressive nationalism, internecine conflicts, perverse effects of transition towards market economy, environmental degradation, etc.[7] This meant four things. First, international peace and security are currently mainly endangered by *intra-state conflicts* rather than by traditional collective security threats (inter-state aggression). Second, collapses of *states* represent a regional and global security threat, with the underlying paradox that extreme weakness could be as dangerous as extreme military capabilities. Third, *non-state actors* are now able (through either terrorism or organized crime, or their interconnection) to seriously endanger the security of nation-states. Fourth, the privileged victims of post-Cold War threats are (in case of genocide, ethnic cleansing and other systematic massacres) *civilian populations*, beginning with ethnic communities. As a consequence, the concept of collective security can no longer be limited to the protection of states; it must include human security concerns so as to encompass peace, development, and human rights.

(b) Responses

The natural reaction of the UN to the changing parameters of international security was a multifaceted use of peace operations, basically for post-conflict rehabilitation and, occasionally, preventative action. However, this instrument was no panacea and demonstrated severe shortcomings in Bosnia-Herzegovina, Somalia, and Rwanda. The UN's self-critical response was the *Brahimi Report* (2000), which contained common sense recommendations without, however, daring (for obvious political reasons) to address the real crux of the matter – that the UN is expected to manage international peace without a standing rapid deployment force and, as a consequence, is compelled more often than not to react too little, too late, or just occasionally. In its *Outcome Document*, the 2005 World Summit referred to the issue through a timid provision calling for the "further development of proposals for enhanced rapidly deployable capacities to reinforce peacekeeping operations in crises" and just hinted at the creation of "an initial operating capability for a standing Police Capacity to provide coherent, effective and responsive start-up capability for the policing component of the U.N. peacekeeping missions and to assist existing missions through the provision of advice and expertise."[8] The *Outcome Document* can, however, be credited for committing states "to take collective action, in a timely and decisive manner, through the Security Council, in accordance with the Charter, including Chapter VII, on a case-by-case basis and in cooperation with relevant regional organizations as appropriate, should peaceful means be inadequate and national authorities manifestly failing to protect their populations from genocide, war crimes, ethnic cleansing and crimes against humanity."[9] Furthermore, it provided for the creation of an intergovernmental Peacebuilding Commission, whose central purpose is to prevent war-torn countries from lapsing back into violence because of inconsistent implementation of peace accords by bringing together all relevant actors to marshal resources and to propose integrated strategies for post-conflict rehabilitation.[10]

(c) Dilemmas and Implications

The adaptation of the UN to the combined effects of multipolarity and the side effects of globalization is clearly incomplete. In addition to a standing rapid deployment force and an interlocking system of peacekeeping capacities enabling the UN to work with regional organizations in complementary partnership, a number of elements are still lacking, inter alia a universal definition of terrorism, a consolidation of the Nuclear Non-Proliferation Treaty regime, and (given the controversy over the American doctrine of preemptive war) clear criteria for the use of force, ruling out unilateralism outside the legitimate boundaries of self-defense.

The unlawful invasion of Iraq (2003), the egregious abuses of human rights committed by the occupying powers and the curtailment of civil rights under the guise of the fight against terrorism in Western democracies introduced a complicating parameter – the oxymoron that international order can also be threatened by the undemocratic behavior of well-established democracies.

(d) Future Trajectories

To borrow a metaphor borrowed from the history of astronomy, the UN is tailor-made for a Ptolemaic type of universe, which has now turned into one of a Copernican-type. A globalizing world needs a strengthened UN, able to respond in a legitimate, credible, and effective way to the daunting challenges of globalization. The 2005

World Summit was meant to address those challenges. It represented a missed opportunity for two main reasons. First, states' nostalgia for old-style sovereignty remains as strong and resilient as ever. As globalization is slowly eroding national sovereignties, all states (big and small) are opposed to a meaningful strengthening of the UN capacities and capabilities. The UN is, so to speak, the scapegoat of globalization. It offers an ideal venue where states can still claim, through imprecatory statements and stands, to be fully sovereign. Second, no meaningful reform can be achieved as long as the US remains, as it presently is, allergic to international law as well as to the UN's basic rules of the game. The doctrinal position of the present US administration is that international law is an à la carte menu from which it can choose and that "the mission determines the coalition," meaning that international organizations are only relevant to the extent that they can be used as occasional members of coalitions of the willing.[11] Although a quantum leap is overdue, most of the UN member states are, for the time being, ready to adopt only petty reforms or perpetuate the *status quo*.

4. Policy Recommendations

1. Effectively empower the UN for the most crucial development-related issues (trade, macroeconomic and adjustment policies, financial crises, etc.).

2. Conduct partnership with the private sector while avoiding the "privatization" of development policies.

3. Establish a standing rapid deployment force at the disposal of the Security Council.

4. Envisage an interlocking system of peacekeeping capacities enabling the UN to work with regional organizations in a complementary manner.

5. Adopt a universal definition of terrorism.

6. Consolidate the Nuclear Non-Proliferation Treaty regime.

7. Elaborate clear criteria for the use of force, ruling out unilateralism outside the legitimate boundaries of self-defense.

References

[1] *The Millennium Assembly of the United Nations*, A/RES/53/202, December 17, 1998.
[2] *We the Peoples: the Role of the U.N. in the 21st Century*, A/54/2000, March 27, 2000, p. 30.
[3] *A More Secure World: Our Shared Responsibility*, A/59/565, December 2, 2004.
[4] *In Larger Freedom: Towards Development, Security and Human Rights for All*, A/59/2005, March 21, 2005, http://www.un.org/largerfreedom/.
[5] For more details on this debate, see J.-P. Thérien, and V. Pouliot, "The Global Compact: Shifting the Politics of International Development," *Global Governance*, Vol. 12, No. 1, 2006, pp. 55-75.
[6] *World Summit Outcome*, United Nations General Assembly, A/RES/60/1, October 24, 2005, pp. 17-68.
[7] However, threats of a military nature are present via the proliferation of weapons of mass destruction and the uncontrolled and excessive accumulation of small arms and light weapons.
[8] United Nations General Assembly, *op. cit.*, note 6, § 92.
[9] *Ibid.*, §139.
[10] *Ibid.*, §§ 97-105.
[11] As admitted by Newt Gingrich, "A limited UN is Best for America," *International Herald Tribune*, September 13, 2005.

CHAPTER 21

EDITORIAL OF POLICY BRIEF ON THE UNITED NATIONS AND THE CHALLENGES OF A GLOBALIZED WORLD: TOWARDS A QUANTUM LEAP FROM MULTILATERALISM TO GLOBALIZATION?

NAYEF R.F. AL-RODHAN

Dr. Nayef R.F. Al-Rodhan is Senior Scholar in Geostrategy and Director of the Program on the Geopolitical Implications of Globalization and Transnational Security at the Geneva Centre for Security Policy, Geneva, Switzerland

1. Review and Critique

As an organization dedicated to the ideals of international law and the most significant global organization, both in terms of membership and scope of its activities,[1] it is vital that the United Nations (UN) adapt to a rapidly changing world. Globalization and the end of the Cold War have significantly altered the environment in which the UN seeks to fulfill its aims and act effectively. Globalization is often perceived as eroding the capacities of sovereign states and elevating the importance of non-state actors. As such, it has important implications for the UN, which embodies the inter-state driven process of multilateralism. The unfamiliar nature of the problems that the organization is likely to face will take it into uncharted waters. If it is to remain relevant and credible, the UN must successfully respond to this changed environment.

Transnational threats to security, such as international terrorism and the proliferation of weapons of mass destruction, increased calls for unilateral, pre-emptive use of force, as well as reservations about the usefulness of the Security Council, are just some of the issues that the UN must face. Indeed, in some quarters, the relevance of the UN is being called into question.

Victor-Yves Ghebali identifies a related challenge facing the UN system.[2] A state-centered, regulatory approach to development is increasingly difficult to maintain, given the steady decline in official development aid, as well as advances in globalization. Involving the private sector in the domain of development offers a possible solution to this problem. Yet, the difficulty will be to marry market goals with the universal ideals of the UN.

Although the UN Charter identifies international peace and security as the organization's major aim, the UN's founders anticipated that collective security would constitute its principal function and activity.[3] Ghebali also argues that a change in the UN's approach to collective security is needed, not as a result of globalization, but as a direct consequence of the end of the Cold War. The demise of the bipolar system has given way to a host of largely non-military, transnational, and intra-state security issues, such as ethnic conflicts, organized criminality, and international terrorism. This means that stability and security involve non-state actors as well as state actors, and intra-state conflict as well as inter-state conflict. As a result, the concept of collective security can no longer be limited to the protection of states, but must also include human security.

This editorial addresses some important implications of globalization and transnational security for the UN. Globalization and a changed international security environment has increased the relevance of both non-state actors and intra-state conflict. The resulting challenges they pose to international organizations, which are the product of a multilateral, inter-state process, are manifold. For whom is the UN supposed to provide security and how it is to achieve these ends needs to be rethought. Equally important, determining how development goals can be effectively met requires a new approach to development and perhaps greater partnership with non-state actors.

2. Dilemmas and Our Recommendations

Globalization and transnational security threats present both opportunities as well as challenges for the United Nations. In order for the UN to retain its relevance and to perform effectively, it needs to address a number of issues linked to its structure as well as its *raison d'être*. We highlight eight dilemmas related to this issue area and eight corresponding recommendations that may contribute to appropriate responses.

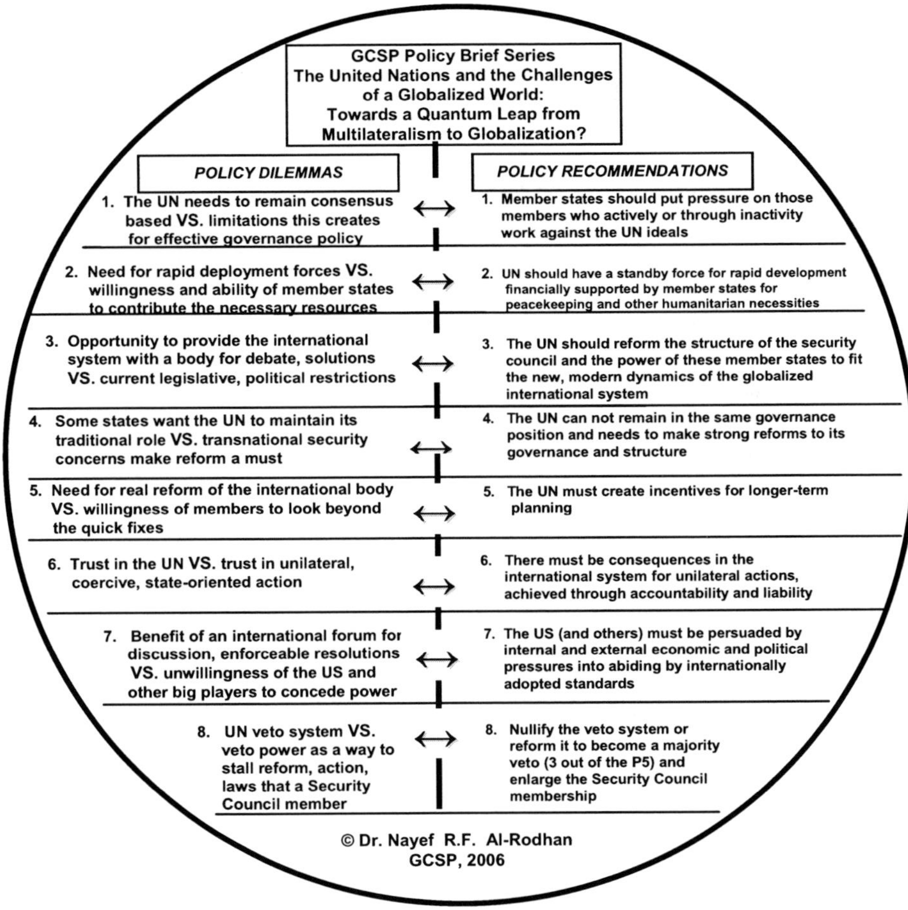

The policy dilemmas and recommendations presented here are directly linked to the challenges currently faced by the UN. One of the most difficult challenges is inadequate political commitment, as well as resources, on the part of member states. While it is easy to criticize the UN for its alleged inefficiency and ineffectiveness, this condition is the product of the will of the states that make up its membership. For instance, the UN ought to have a rapid reaction force for peacekeeping and humanitarian assistance, but financial and political constraints currently prevent it from developing such a force.

Another dilemma is related to the need for reform. Some commentators and governments argue that the UN should maintain its traditional role, while others call for a shift in its focus to include greater emphasis on transnational security threats. It is our belief that the UN must be reformed, both in terms of its governance capacities and its structure. The UN structure, after all, reflects the context in which the organization was established. As the supreme decision-making structure, the Security Council mirrors the unequal distribution of power that existed when the UN Charter was signed following World War II. The five major victors – the United States, the United Kingdom, France, the Soviet Union/Russia, and China – are permanent members of the Security Council ("P5"), while ten additional seats rotate among the other members. Each of the P5 has the right to veto actions considered by the Council. The Security Council is, therefore, skewed in favor of the powers that emerged victorious from World War II.[4] The UN veto system ought to be dismantled or reformed to become a majority veto system and the Security Council membership should be enlarged.

In addition, the unwillingness of member states to abide by UN resolutions is weakening and seriously damaging the credibility of the institution. A major obstacle to ensuring the effectiveness of the UN in today's world is that some states are tempted to take unilateral actions that undermine the organization. States should be persuaded through internal and external economic and political pressures to abide by internationally agreed standards and obligations. For this to occur, punitive actions against states engaging in harmful unilateralism should, for example, be taken.

3. Conclusion

Globalization and transnational challenges to security present a number of challenges for all international organizations, the UN not withstanding. The UN represents a multilateral and, thus, inter-state process, in which non-state actors and security issues that are not confined to the state are gaining in relevance. As a result, the UN needs to decide how best to respond to world development needs, while also serving the ends of peace and security.

References

[1] B. Russett, H. Starr and D. Kinsella, *World Politics: The Menu for Choice*, seventh edition (Belmont, CA, etc.: Thomson and Wadsworth, 2004), p. 299.
[2] For the brief in its entirety, please see Chapter 20.
[3] Russett, et. al., *op. cit.,* note 1, p. 305.
[4] *Ibid.*, p. 300.

CHAPTER 22

INFORMATION TECHNOLOGY, TERRORISM, AND GLOBAL SECURITY

MARC FINAUD

Mr. Marc Finaud is Faculty Member at the Geneva Centre for Security Policy, Geneva, Switzerland

Abstract
The information technology (IT) revolution that the world has been experiencing over the last two decades has had a significant impact not only on the world economy but also on global security, and in particular on international terrorism. Indeed, IT advances have allowed terrorists to gain easy access to sensitive information, spread their ideology, recruit supporters or operatives, plan and carry out their operations, and conduct criminal activities. IT networks can also offer targets for terrorists who aim to disrupt or destroy critical infrastructure by launching cyber-attacks. But IT can also be exploited by governments as a counterterrorism and an intelligence tool: it permits the surveillance of potentially malicious groups, the detection of planned attacks, the mitigation of eventual attacks, and can facilitate the countering of ideological support for terrorism. Some progress has already been made in raising awareness of risks and levels of preparedness, but there is a need for more international cooperation and public-private partnership in harmonizing legislation, improving the security of cyberspace, and promoting better law enforcement.

1. Policy Challenges

The revolution in the field of information technology (IT) that the world has witnessed over the past two decades has accelerated and kept pace with the process of globalization. Developments in information and communications technology (ICT) have been characterized by increasingly greater speeds of data transmission, increased capacity for data storage, more mobility, and the integration of various functions. The results of this evolution on a global scale, especially in terms of economic impact, have exceeded most predictions. A 2002 forecast of the annual growth of world ICT spending (hardware, software, and services) for 2003-2007 was updated in 2005 from 8 percent to nearly 10 percent (over 12 percent for Europe, the Middle East, and Africa). This spending grew from $2.1 trillion in 2001 to $3 trillion in 2005 and is expected to reach $3.7 trillion in 2008. Its share of world GDP reached 7.4 percent in 2001 and is now stable at around 7 percent.[1] ICT spending will total $15 trillion in the present decade, as compared to $6 trillion during the first 40 years of the existence of such technology.[2] Globally, Internet usage increased more than fourfold from 2000 to 2005,[3] with the total number of users exceeding one billion in 2005.[4] In spite of the "digital divide" between developed economies (with 300 secure e-commerce servers for every 1 million people) and developing nations (with only two secure e-commerce servers for every 1 million people), the latter have considerably increased their access to ICT: between 1980 and 2005, the number of telephone subscribers in developing countries increased thirty fold, reaching a world share of 60 percent, against 20 percent in 1980, thanks to their "leapfrogging" in mobile telephony.[5]

Developments on such a scale could not but have an impact on security, one of the conditions influencing how economies develop and what policies states implement. If the "new economy" is increasingly dependent on ICT, then ICT infrastructure can certainly be the target or conduit of hostile actions. Thus, in addition to being a major factor in terms of growth, ICT can also cause certain vulnerabilities. International terrorism has become one of the main challenges to global security. It is not surprising that this phenomenon used all the advances offered by IT to thrive, thus exacerbating challenges for decision makers tasked with ensuring national security.

(a) The IT revolution has helped the development of terrorism

(i) IT facilitates access to sensitive information of interest to terrorist groups

Transparency is a fundamental element of any democratic society. With this comes the right of citizens to have access to information, with certain limitations on the grounds of national security. The widespread use of ICT has made the regulation of such access and related limitations more difficult to enforce. Moreover, the academic community, the force behind the initial development of information sharing through the Internet, at times overlooks the risk of the ill-intentioned use of this information. There are numerous websites that explain ways of producing explosives or weapons of mass destruction (WMD) in terms that are accessible to people with an average level of expertise.[6] Even websites that are intended to warn and prepare people against the use of such explosives or weapons contain information that may be of direct interest to terrorists.[7] Aerial and satellite images and maps of critical infrastructure can also be found on the Internet. It was revealed in March 2006 that the names of thousands of covert CIA operatives are available in Internet databases.[8]

(ii) IT allows terrorist groups to spread their ideology and facilitates recruitment

Cyberspace experts now talk of a "virtual caliphate" of some 4,000 pro-Al-Qaida websites, blogs, and chat rooms disseminating *jihadist* messages or propaganda.[9] These are used for training; recruitment; disseminating tactics, techniques, procedures; financing (through Internet pay sites); and garnering support. By spreading propaganda and showing videos of executions of hostages or successful strikes, the Internet contributes to the radicalization of young Muslims.[10]

(iii) Terrorists use IT tools to plan and carry out operations

The attackers of September 11, 2001, used the Internet to plan their operations by booking air tickets online and communicating with one another through Internet-based telephone services and chat rooms. It has also been reported that some terrorist groups use sophisticated technological devices such as optoelectronics, encrypted communications equipment, global positioning systems (GPS), and remote electronic bomb detonators.[11] Al-Qaida computers seized in Afghanistan contained models of dams and computer programs that could have been useful in attacks against such infrastructure.[12] Here again, law enforcement personnel are handicapped by the accessibility, versatility, speed, and transnational character of cyberspace, which allows almost total impunity.

(iv) The possibility of computer attacks by terrorists against critical infrastructure or information networks is real

Although it has not yet materialized and the possibility is debated by experts, one cannot disregard the risk that terrorist groups will use IT not only as a weapon but also as a target, e.g., by launching cyber-attacks against supervisory control and data acquisition (SCADA) systems and networks controlling sensitive infrastructure (air-traffic control systems, power grids, dams, industrial plants or nuclear installations, communications systems, financial services, etc.) or computers containing critical data. At this stage, this is more the domain of individual or organized "hackers, crackers, and hacktivists" acting on the basis of personal, economic, ideological, or criminal motives. But if the activity of these individuals is an natural by-product of an IT society, it is an increasingly worrying phenomenon. In 1988, only six incidents of hacking were reported to the Carnegie-Mellon University Computer Emergency Response Team (CERT); in 2001, this number reached 52,658.[13] In 2002, Computer Economics Inc. estimated the annual cost to the United States (US) economy of computer virus and worm attacks to be $17 billion.[14] If terrorist networks acquire the necessary skills, opting for cyber-attacks would be only a matter of strategic choice. Inferring from their past behavior, one can predict that they would not hesitate to use IT to target critical infrastructure if it allowed them to attain their objectives: massive fatalities and/or major disruption of economic, political, and social life in the targeted country, either independently or in conjunction with a physical attack, and subsequent widespread media coverage.

(v) Terrorist groups and organized crime often use opportunities offered by IT

International terrorists and organized criminal groups both use IT advances, such as encryption or anonymizer features on computers, and hire highly qualified hacking specialists of these systems who conduct their transnational operations without fear of detection.[15] Terrorist groups often conduct additional criminal activities of their own, such as money laundering, trafficking in drugs or human beings, credit card fraud, and selling counterfeit goods, in order to fund their organizations. Just like multinational corporations, terrorist groups capitalize on the advantages of Western societies (openness, IT development) and those of developing countries (legislative loopholes, weak law enforcement, corruption, cheap labor).[16] They use the Internet to produce forged identity documents for themselves, their operatives, or the people they smuggle into Western countries. They enjoy the flexibility of electronic fund transfers and covert banking. The challenge for governments is to increase the legal and technical obstacles standing in the way of those activities in order to make law enforcement more effective.

(b) IT can be used by governments as a counterterrorism and intelligence instrument
In 2003, the United States[17] identified several areas where the use of IT was critical to the fight against terrorism: prevention, detection, and mitigation of terrorist attacks. In addition, IT can be of invaluable assistance in countering ideological support for terrorism.

(i) IT can help in the prevention of terrorist attacks
Prior to any potential terrorist attack, law enforcement and intelligence services rely heavily on the surveillance of electronic communications and Internet use to identify significant patterns of behavior among suspected groups or individuals. Techniques have been developed for modeling the evolution of social groups in Web chat rooms, newsgroups, and bulletin boards, with the specific goal of detecting potentially harmful groups.[18] Progress made in information fusion, i.e. the aggregation of data from various sources, combined with powerful search engines, may enable well-equipped and properly trained specialists to uncover terrorist plans.

(ii) IT can help security services detect an imminent terrorist attack
The collection and rapid analysis of intelligence through electronic means can prove critical in detecting and attributing planned terrorist attacks. The failure of the US intelligence community to properly interpret the signals it received prior to the September 11 attacks was one of the main flaws criticized by the 9/11 Commission, which led to the reorganization of the US intelligence architecture. On the other hand, excessive reliance by the US intelligence community on electronic signals prior to the invasion of Iraq, in light of subsequent revelations about the absence of WMD and the underestimated insurgency, was another failure.

(iii) The use and protection of IT are crucial in mitigating and managing the consequences of a terrorist attack
Emergency first responders (fire-fighters, police, paramedics, other health-care workers, etc.) need to be able to have confidence in the capacity of their IT systems to allow for their communications, coordination, and information sharing. For such agencies, the

challenge is to keep their systems up-to-date and protected from attacks, to train their staff adequately how to use such systems, and to share good practices and lessons learned with other agencies. Private businesses also need support from governments to increase their resilience to terrorist attacks.[19]

(iv) The use of IT is necessary to raise awareness of risks and to counter ideological support for terrorism
Governments can take advantage of the vast spectrum of opportunities offered by the digital revolution to increase knowledge and awareness among the public of the terrorist risk. They can use official websites or create dedicated websites to publicize information about threats, encourage the public to report incidents, and engage the various communities of stakeholders (academia, the business world, civil society). Governments can also seek allies among the same groups targeted by terrorists for recruitment or support as a part of their own counterterrorism policy. Indeed, *jihadism* is more an internal struggle among extremist and moderate Muslims than a clash of civilizations between the West and the Muslim world.[20]

2. Responses

Reminiscent of the arms race during the Cold War, the world is now witnessing a similar contest between terrorist groups on the one hand, which try to exploit the potential of IT for their own purposes, and governments and international organizations on the other hand, which try to harness the power of IT to prevent terrorist acts before they happen. The temptation exists to deal with this threat on a national basis, while it clearly requires international cooperation.

(a) Until now, most efforts have focused on preventing cyber-attacks:
The 2003 US National Strategy to Secure Cyberspace, designed by the new Department of Homeland Security,[21] details a policy aimed at preventing cyber-attacks against critical US infrastructure, reducing vulnerabilities to attacks, and improving preparedness for possible attacks. The European Union adopted in 2005 a Framework Decision on Attacks against Information Systems,[22] which provides for harmonized penalties applicable to cyber-criminals and a 24/7 Network of operational points of contact for exchanging data on

attacks against information systems. Since 2001, Interpol's High Tech Crime Unit has been implementing an early-warning system consisting of national specialized contact officers for standardized police communication.[23]

(b) The international community needs to improve IT-based counterterrorism tools and prevention through law enforcement cooperation

Law enforcement and intelligence agencies still have difficulties in successfully detecting, tracking, identifying, and neutralizing terrorist groups, which benefit from the anonymity of cyberspace. The IT industry is reluctant to let governments regulate the Internet or strengthen standards on its use, and companies fear for their image if they report incidents.[24] However, a public-private partnership, as part of a single national architecture, is required to agree on measures that would be both efficient and acceptable in terms of privacy, such as improving the resilience of Internet protocols, extending record-keeping rules for Internet service providers, or developing filtering systems for forged source addresses. The international harmonization of criminal legislation also appears to be indispensable in order to plug existing loopholes used by terrorist groups. The Council of Europe's 2001 Convention on Cyber Crime[25] was recommended as a model by the 2005 Interpol Conference on Cyber Crime,[26] but the progress made so far in this direction has been minimal. The Internet Governance Forum, to be convened in November 2006 under the auspices of the UN,[27] will have a heavy workload in this respect.

3. Dilemmas

Governments and decision makers are confronted with the following dilemmas:

1. How to prevent the spread of information useful to terrorists and at the same time promote the dissemination of information needed for public awareness and preparedness;

2. How to reconcile some control of means of communication with freedom of speech, which can be abused to promote violence, racial hatred, or religious intolerance;

3. How to strike the proper balance between the need to preserve privacy and efficiency in counterterrorism; and

4. How to strike the right balance between electronic and human intelligence as a source of information in countering terrorism.

4. Implications

1. If governments want to reduce terrorists' access to sensitive information, they need to explain the risks and convince the public of what is necessary. A culture of vigilance must be part of the training of all staff involved in making information available.

2. Enacting or adapting legislation to make the spread of racial hatred or incitement to violence a criminal offense would impose new constraints on terrorist groups. The 2003 Additional Protocol to the Council of Europe's Convention on Cyber Crime[28] offers a model, but there are still fundamental differences between the approaches taken by Europe and the US, with the latter being more reluctant to hinder freedom of speech.

3. If governments decide to reduce civil liberties in the name of the fight against terrorism, this needs to be publicly debated and decided on the basis of a broad consensus. This has been illustrated by recent debates in the United States about the wiretapping of private communications without a court order; in Britain and France about government demands on Internet service providers or telephone companies to keep records for a longer period; as well as by the transatlantic dispute over the ECHELON interception network.[29]

4. Increased recourse to electronic intelligence requires adequate investment in new technologies, research and development, and training. If human intelligence is to retain its importance, there should be investment in analysis capacity.

5. Future Trajectories/Scenarios

Future scenarios, based on such technological advances as the expansion of broadband Internet, 3G/4G mobile phones, multimedia messaging, wireless technology, will only exacerbate the existing race between terrorists and law enforcement officials. On the one hand, the more the global economy becomes dependent on IT, the more it becomes vulnerable. On the other hand, further technological advances may also result in progress in the surveillance and detection capacity of intelligence and law enforcement agencies.

6. Policy Recommendations

Governments should:

1. Adopt a national strategy, where such a strategy does not exist, for countering the use of IT by terrorists, based on a broad national consensus and distribution of tasks among stakeholders;

2. Encourage and invest in scientific research and industrial development of IT systems that are more resistant to terrorist use and facilitate law enforcement agencies to combat these illegal acts by implementing current legislation and providing these agencies in countries that do not have the means for acquiring and supporting them.

3. Harmonize anti-terrorism legislation on an international level, on the basis of Council of Europe conventions, in order to deprive terrorists of loopholes that can be exploited.

4. Cooperate with developing countries in designing adequate legislation on both terrorism and organized crime and in strengthening law enforcement capacities to combat both phenomena.

References

1 "Digital Planet 2004 Update – The Global Information Economy," World Information Technology and Services Alliance (WITSA), October 2005, http://www.witsa.org/digitalplanet/DigitalPlanet2004Update_execsummary.pdf.

2 J. Gantz, Chief Research Officer, IDC, "Information Technology: An Engine for Global Economic Growth," April 16, 2002, Microsoft, http://www.microsoft.com/presspass/features/2002/apr02/04-16glcqa.mspx.

3 World Bank, "Information and Communication for Development 2006 – Global Trends and Policies," http://siteresources.worldbank.org/EXTINFORMATIONANDCOMMUNICATIONANDTECHNOLOGIES/Resources/282822-1141851022286/IC4D-Summary.pdf.

4 http://www.internetworldstats.com/stats.htm.

5 World Bank , *op. cit.,* note 3.

6 See, for example, the website of the Federation of American Scientists: http://www.fas.org/nuke/intro/index.html.

7 See the website of "WMD First Responders," which includes all the available literature in English on WMD risks and measures to take either in dissemination prevention or in case of attack: http://www.wmdfirstresponders.com/.

8 http://www.chicagotribune.com/news/nationworld/chi-060311ciamain-story,1,123362.story?ctrack=1&cset=true.

9 A. de Borchgrave, Director, Transnational Threats, Center for Strategic and International Studies (CSIS), "Evolving Counterterrorism Strategy," Subcommittee on International Terrorism and Nonproliferation, US House of Representatives, October 28, 2005, http://wwwc.house.gov/international_relations/109/bor092905.pdf.

10 CENTCOM Senior Leaders Talking Points, February 1, 2006, http://ics.leeds.ac.uk/papers/vp01.cfm?outfit=pmt&folder=2558&paper=2592.

11 "Computer Attack and Cyber Terrorism – Vulnerabilities and Policy Issues for Congress," CRS Report, October 17, 2003, http://www.fas.org/irp/crs/RL32114.pdf.

12 *Ibid.*

13 E. Gelbstein and A. Kamal, "Information Insecurity – A Survival Guide to the Uncharted Territories of Cyber-Threats and Cyber-Security," United Nations ICT Task Force, September 2002, p. 17.

14 *Ibid.*

15 L.I. Shelley, "Organized Crime, Terrorism and Cybercrime," in A. Bryden, P. Fluri (eds.), *Security Sector Reform: Institutions, Society and Good Governance*, (Zürich: 2003), see http://www.american.edu/traccc/resources/publications/shelle31.pdf.

16 *Ibid.*

17 "Information Technology for Counterterrorism: Immediate Actions and Future Possibilities," http://bob.nap.edu/html/IT_counterterror/.

18 http://www.cs.rpi.edu/news/stories/story-04152004a.html.

19 A Resilience Benchmark Survey was conducted by the UK financial service tripartite authorities in London after the July 2005 attacks, showing that the IT systems of financial companies were resilient and that their recovery time was short, but that there was a need for a better understanding of interdependencies with suppliers and counterparties, as well as for guidance on good practices. See http://www.fsc.gov.uk/upload/public/Files/9/Web%20-%20Res%20Bench%20Report%2020051214.pdf.

20 See, for instance, the initiative of Yusuf al-Qaradawi, a Qatar-based Egyptian religious scholar, to establish websites and networks promoting a cosmopolitan interpretation of Islam: P. Mandaville, "Toward a Virtual Caliphate: Al-Qaeda is not the Only Muslim Group Harnessing the Power of Globalization," *YaleGlobal*, October 27, 2005, http://yaleglobal.yale.edu/display.article?id=6416.

21 http://www.us-cert.gov/reading_room/cyberspace_strategy.pdf.

22 http://register.consilium.eu.int/pdf/en/04/st15/st15010.en04.pdf.

23 http://www.interpol.int/public/icpo/pressreleases/pr2003/pr200331.asp.

---

[24] H.N. Miller, “Cyber Attacks: Removing Roadblocks to Investigation and Information Sharing,” statement before the US Senate Committee on the Judiciary, March 28, 2000, http://www.itaa.org/eweb/upload/CyberAttacks3-2000.pdf.

[25] http://conventions.coe.int/Treaty/en/Treaties/Html/185.htm.

[26] http://www.interpol.int/Public/TechnologyCrime/Conferences/6thIntConf/Resolution.asp.

[27] http://www.un.org/apps/news/story.asp?NewsID=17534&Cr=internet&Cr1=.

[28] http://conventions.coe.int/Treaty/en/Treaties/Html/189.htm.

[29] See the 2001 report of the European Parliament on ECHELON: http://www.fas.org/irp/program/process/rapport_echelon_en.pdf.

CHAPTER 23

EDITORIAL OF POLICY BRIEF ON INFORMATION TECHNOLOGY, TERRORISM, AND GLOBAL SECURITY

NAYEF R.F. AL-RODHAN

Dr. Nayef R.F. Al-Rodhan is Senior Scholar in Geostrategy and Director of the Program on the Geopolitical Implications of Globalization and Transnational Security at the Geneva Centre for Security Policy, Geneva, Switzerland

1. Review and Critique

The introduction of a new technology into a society can have a profound impact on its structure and development. Over the past fifteen years, we have seen the impact that the Internet has had on global society. Communication has taken on a new significance, as traditional means have given way to the era of Internet telephony, instant messaging, and 3G technology. While it is only natural that governments and political entities benefit from such technology, they also face new challenges as a result of it.

One of these challenges is the impact that such technology has on the ability of terrorists to recruit members, spread their ideologies, and plan and launch attacks around the world. New technologies provide clear advantages in the ease of communication. Unfortunately, this is the same ease in the case of peaceful purposes as for coordination in the terrorist domain. At the same time, however, technology also provides government and law enforcement agencies with the ability to monitor terrorist activities with greater awareness. So while the technology offers a global venue for terrorist groups, it also grants authorities the tools with which to combat illegal operations.

The era of cyber-crime is developing faster than most regulatory bodies are able to react. Mobile telephony provides a great opportunity for growth in both the private and public sectors. However, it also connects the world in a way that has never been the case previously. It allows for messages, both well-intentioned and not, to be transmitted in a matter of seconds. How are these challenges being dealt with and what are the current responses to them?

Marc Finaud outlines two major challenges posed by states with regard to information technology (IT) and terrorism.[1] The first is that "the IT revolution has helped the development of terrorism." Second, he argues that "IT can be used by governments as a counterterrorism and intelligence instrument." In terms of the development of terrorism, he convincingly argues that the Internet provides an easily accessible resource for distributing sensitive information, such as how to construct bombs or purchase weapons. In addition, the use of computers as a recruitment tool and as a means of attacking targets through cyberspace is a real threat, which Finaud gives due credibility. He provides sound justification for the use of IT in countering terrorism and concludes that proper utilization of such tools can be a means of properly managing such threats.

The policy brief addresses a vital part of the globalization debate. As the Internet connects communities and countries, this connectivity opens itself up to information sharing, which can lead to positive developments but can also open the door for dissemination of harmful information and accessibility to government systems. When utilized properly, this technology also provides solutions to dealing with such issues.

2. Dilemmas and Our Recommendations

The introduction of new technologies presents both challenges and opportunities for states. The development of new policies concerning use of the Internet and other technologies by terrorists is fiercely debated in policy and academic circles. Government agencies and states will need such policies in the years to come to properly handle these challenges and dilemmas. How best to regulate these matters has been widely discussed in recent years, yet determining the best way to move forward, especially in the entire international system, is much more difficult. This is an extremely important task since it will require transnational cooperation and cross-border regulations. Presented here are eight dilemmas in this area and corresponding recommendations for appropriate policy responses.

The policy dilemmas and recommendations that appear here are clearly issues that states are currently facing in terms of information technology and the utilization of such technologies by terrorists. The most noteworthy of these dilemmas and recommendations involve balancing the proper level of privacy with civil liberties. In order to solve this dilemma, states must ensure a balance of policies and monitoring that is transparent enough to guarantee the preservation of civil liberties. One other major dilemma facing states is the lack of coherence in the security of systems both on the commercial and governmental levels. For industries that operate within security-sensitive areas such as airlines, measures should be implemented that make certain that a level of security exists that can prevent a breach.

In addition, states face issues of balancing freedom of speech and state censorship. Policies must be developed that respect this fundamental freedom while regulating offensive and dangerous sites. This is also important in the monitoring of good, peaceful messages versus harmful and radical messages. States must create international regulations and organizations that can monitor the creation of websites and the information traffic that passes through them. A widening of the information-sharing network is also key in utilizing technology as a means of fighting terrorism, in the form of cyber-crime, as well as in other cases.

Finally, states and policy makers must find a way to solve problems related to the speed in which information is spread, which leads to shortened response times. The development of effective and real-time response mechanisms and policy solutions by governments is the most efficient way to move forward in this area. Without it, shortened response times can be a crucial flaw in any response that is developed.

3. Conclusion

The international system greatly benefits from the technological advances that the Internet and other new information tools provide. The connectivity made possible by these developments in technology brings us closer to those whose interests contribute to global security and stability, as well as to those whose interests do not. An important challenge is how to encourage states to create harsher penalties for the misuse of this technology, as well as to provide incentives for furthering international cooperation in combating this phenomenon.

References

[1] For the brief in its entirety, please see Chapter 22.

CHAPTER 24

IDENTIFYING TRANSCULTURAL SOLUTIONS FOR OUR GLOBALIZED WORLD

NAYEF R.F. AL-RODHAN

Dr. Nayef R.F. Al-Rodhan is Senior Scholar in Geostrategy and Director of the Program on the Geopolitical Implications of Globalization and Transnational Security at the Geneva Centre for Security Policy, Geneva, Switzerland

Conclusion

Throughout this publication, we have focused on the transcultural aspects of security and stability. In assessing topics such as migration, xenophobia in the media, ethics and civil liberties, the changing role of the United Nations (UN), and the security impact of informal remittance flows, we have identified some general themes and established links between various policy recommendations. These brief concluding thoughts will highlight some of these linkages and illustrate how policy-making processes can work towards furthering global peace and stability.

One of the major themes that emerge from the discourse on any of these topics is the idea of political and economic preference or stereotyping that is addressed in a number of different forms in the contributions to this volume. Most notably, it can be found in the chapters dealing with oil, ports, and steel issues, but it is also an important theme in the migration brief, in Fraser Cameron's discussion of transcultural issues in Europe, in the question of the European Union's acceptance of Turkey as a member, in the assessment of the scandal involving blasphemous cartoons in Denmark, as well as in the chapter on current ethical practices and civil liberties throughout the world. In each of these cases, a state or group of people has created a problem or furthered existing societal tensions by granting preferential treatment to one group or stereotyping another community based on religion or nationality. The obvious conclusion is that inclusiveness and tolerance would provide amenable solutions in a number of these policy challenges.

Of course, these values and their application cannot be easily translated into national policy, nor do we intend to base our entire concluding thoughts of these transnational issues solely on this assumption. However, if states would work to implement policies and practices that promote diversity and multi-cultural communities, this could provide a foundation for peace to resolve a number of these issues before they even reach policy agendas. By implementing such policies, governments would already find themselves comfortably on the path towards a more stable and secure future.

Globalization as a process and as a global force is re-creating communities, and more importantly, is re-shaping the way in which communities view themselves and other groups of people. As globalization impacts the operation of the UN and other intergovernmental organizations, the way in which states operate will also change. As the world becomes more technologically dependent, opportunities for criminal activity also increase and improve, and so must our defenses.

The recommendations put forth by our authors share some common themes worth identifying here. First of all, they are based on the notion that while globalization presents challenges to our established norms and operations, it also enables state structures and businesses to find the means to make our world more secure. The developments in information technology are an obvious example. While dependence on technology and internet systems creates vulnerabilities, it also enables states and law enforcement institutions to monitor and track criminal activities more effectively than ever before. In each of the subjects discussed in this publication, it is just as important to identify and utilize the opportunities presented by globalization as to face the challenges it presents.

Second, states, intergovernmental organizations, as well as non-governmental organizations need to take a more cooperative approach to developing transnational policies to handle transnational threats and challenges. These organizations should work to develop policies that are useful at the state level, but concurrently provide policy cohesion at the international level. Without streamlining processes, particularly in the tracking and sharing of information on criminal activity, it will be impossible to adopt and implement any transnational solutions, which are urgently required, as demonstrated in a number of the briefs in this book.

Third, politicians must win public support for and retain the trust of the public in their policies. This is particularly true for the issues of migration, and ethics and civil liberties. In both cases, political leaders must enjoy public confidence if order and political stability are to prevail in the long term. The same applies to peacekeeping operations: The forces that are deployed in a particular area must win the trust of the public in order for their mission to be successful.

To conclude, globalization is changing the way that communities interact with other communities and with governments, as well the composition of their internal structures. This, in turn, affects the way that states interact and therefore the structure, stability, and security of the entire international system. When intolerance, xenophobia, stereotyping, discrimination, and hatred thrive, security and stability cannot be maintained in the short- or long-term future of any state or community. These insights should be included in any comprehensive security strategy that aims to build long-term transcultural security and stability.

INDEX